HOW TO MASTER

YOUR EMOTIONS

The Best Guide to Improve Your Emotional Intelligence. Learn To Master Your Feelings, Overcome Your Negativity, And Improve Your Social Skills to Read People's Emotions

Luke J. Hamilton

Table of Contents

Introduction

Emotions are a powerful and fundamental part of our well-being. This is because being the driving force in our everyday lives, emotions shape our ways of thinking, behaviors, as well as overall character, and they influence how we relate and socialize with others. Since they are innate by nature, they are most of the time very difficult to break free from. This book seeks to help readers to further understand emotions and how to go about the different manifestations and baggage, which come with them. Whether positive or negative, emotions have a way of affecting our lives with ripple effects, which can last for longer periods.

Life is an extremely tough journey. At times you get to the point where you ask yourself whether you will make it or not. Many people give up, while others postpone their plans just because things haven't gonged the right way. The sad thing is that success and failure are all engraved in the mind. The way you handle emotions and attitudes will determine whether you succeed or you fail. Just like anything else, anything you do takes practice and a lot of patience.

Through practice, you can learn to master your emotions. When you do this, you will be able to manage what is pleasant and what is unpleasant. Before you can get to this level, you need first to recognize the emotions and then label them. Give them a name and a size.

When you have time to master your emotions, you will find life being better and easier than it is at the moment. Make haste when choosing the right way to master emotions, because any slip and you will end up losing it.

We talk about mastering your emotions in this book. We look at the various emotions that you can have and how they impact your life. At the end of the book, you will understand what it means to be emotionally intelligent and why it is vital for you to master your emotions the right way.

How do we change our emotions, and is it really possible to do so? How can one transition from negative emotions to more positive ones, what will be the overall impact of such an action in your life and relation with others, including your surrounding? Are you also capable of maintaining this newfound feeling to the end? This is a very powerful change that is also worth looking at in a broader sense. Because emotions blow hot and cold sometimes, what are the short and long-term solutions to addressing each segment, without ever feeling burdened? Above all, it is also very vital for us to look at ways of growing our emotions. How can we also handle positive emotions without being overwhelmed by them? As it is not only the negative ones that can bring great emotional baggage. Rather, even positive ones as well. How do you go about the negative feelings of worry and stress, when you lack motivation in your life? What do you do when you are full of fear, panic, resentment, anger and rage, and on the path towards self-destruction?

This book will help you find ways of rescuing yourself from the shackles of any negative emotions that might threaten to tear you apart making you feel useless as a result. By reading this book, you will become a better person very much capable of having a very positive attitude towards life, no matter the situation you find yourself in.

"The emotions can be characterized as a positive or negative experience that is related to a specific example of physiological movement." Emotions produce diverse physiological, social, and intellectual changes. The first job of emotions was to rouse versatile practices that in the past would have added to the passing on of qualities through survival, proliferation, and family selection.

Emotions include various parts, for example, emotional experience, subjective procedures, expressive conduct, psychophysiological changes, and instrumental conduct. At one time, many scholars endeavored to distinguish the emotions of a test subject: William James with an emotional encounter, behaviorists with instrumental conduct, psychophysiologists with physiological changes, etc. All the more as of late, emotion is said to comprise a considerable number of segments. The various parts of emotion are arranged to some degree diversely relying upon the scholarly order. In brain science and reasoning, emotion commonly incorporates an abstract, cognizant encounter described essentially by psychophysiological articulations, organic responses, and mental states. A comparative multi-componential depiction of emotion is found in humanism. For instance, Peggy Thoits depicted emotions as including physiological segments, social or passionate marks (outrage, shock, and so forth), expressive body activities, and the examination of circumstances and settings.

For what reason do we all of the sudden encounter emotions that we were not anticipating? To this and more questions you can find answers through this book

Chapter 1.   What Are Emotions?

It can often be too easy to let emotional health fall through the cracks as we weave through our hectic and complicated lives, letting negative feelings run rampant while we count every second of that rare moment of contentment. Or perhaps, you're less concerned with feeling happy than you are with feeling anything at all after years of suppressing your emotions, consciously hiding how you feel. Wherever your emotional distress comes from, understand that emotions make us human, but they do not define who we are.

It is okay to be confused or overwhelmed by your emotions; you are *not* immature, *not* weak, and *not* stupid for experiencing emotional turmoil. All too often, we see our emotional turmoil as a sign of inadequacy, but you are not inadequate, and you are not alone. We all have our own personal emotional struggles, and anyone can become lost in the storms they create. Understand that we're all confused, sometimes. What matters is that you're trying, and if you're reading this book, you already are.

Even scientists, psychologists, and professionals in the study of thoughts and emotion struggle to define and understand emotions because they are so difficult to observe and measure. Every individual's emotions are subjective to his or her own experiences, beliefs, thoughts, and reactions, and everyone interacts with the world in different ways.

What's more, emotions rarely manifest as single, distinct feelings. Instead, they oftentimes present simultaneously or one as the result of another, forming a confusing conglomeration of several emotions that language fails to express.

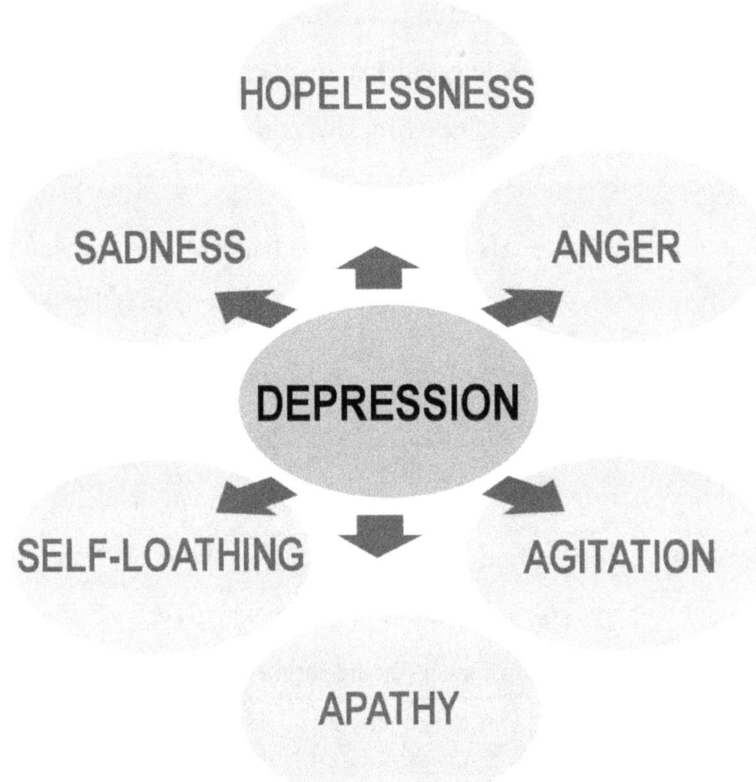

Your emotional self is a complex being, but there is no one better suited to understanding your emotions than you are. You can begin to overcome intense negative emotions by learning to recognize and understand what you are feeling and why.

What Exactly Are Emotions?

If I asked you to create a list of emotions, that would be easy, right? There's joy, amusement, awe, sadness, grief, anger, jealousy, fear, shame, and on and on you could go. There are many names for the feelings you experience, but these names are just words, nominatives that fail to fully represent the complicated and subjective sensations you deal with on a regular basis. What, exactly, do these words mean? What is happening inside your mind and body when you experience a positive emotion like love or a negative emotion like anxiety?

Even psychological and scientific professionals debate the definition of emotion, some making clear distinctions between "emotion" and "feeling" and "mood" while others focus on the chemical sources of emotions. I encourage you to research these methodologies on your own if you are interested in learning more about theory, but for this book, I'm going to keep it simple. I will use words like "feeling" and "emotion" interchangeably to mean the raw, indefinable sensations that arise from inside, affecting our thoughts, responses, and behaviors.

All too often, it is difficult to even name the feeling being experienced, making emotional distress all the more intense. Perhaps, this list of simple definitions and some common symptoms will help you identify some of your own negative emotions.

Fear/Panic - A response to perceived danger, physical or emotional

- PERSPIRATION
- COLD SENSATIONS
- DIZZINESS
- HYPERVENTILATION
- INCREASED HEART AND BREATH RATES

Anxiety/Worry - Apprehension, pessimism, or a general sense of unease

- STOMACH AND/OR CHEST PAIN
- MUSCLE TENSION AND/OR PAIN
- CHANGES IN APPETITE
- CHANGES IN SLEEP QUALITY

Anger/Rage - A hostile response to a perceived offense; irritability

- INCREASED HEART AND BREATH RATES
- SURGE OF ADRENALINE
- DECREASED ABILITY TO THINK CLEARLY
- LACK OF SELF-RESTRAINT
- EXPLOSIVE OUTBURSTS

Irritability - General state of aggravation, frustration; prone to anger

- BECOMING EASILY UPSET/ANGRY
- INCREASED HEART RATE

- CONFUSION AND/OR AGGRESSION

Agitation - General state of irritability; inability to calm thoughts or sit still

- RACING THOUGHTS
- MUSCLE TENSION AND/OR PAIN
- EASILY BECOMING UPSET

Jealousy - Insecurity over perceived lack of something

- SENSE OF LOW SELF-ESTEEM/SELF-WORTH
- FEELINGS OF INFERIORITY
- FEELINGS OF RESENTMENT

Sadness/Greif - A condition of despair, perceived disadvantage, loss

- URGE TO CRY
- SENSE OF HELPLESSNESS
- FATIGUE/LETHARGY
- FEELINGS OF LONELINESS

Depression - Severe sensations of despondency and/or sadness

- A GENERALLY DEPRESSED MOOD/STATE OF BEING
- FEELING WORTHLESS OR HELPLESS
- LOSS OF INTEREST, ENERGY, FOCUS, AND/OR PLEASURE
- INCREASE OR DECREASE IN APPETITE
- THOUGHTS OF DEATH OR SUICIDE

Apathy - Indifference, lack of feeling

- LOSS OF INTEREST

- LOSS OF CONCERN
- FEELINGS OF BEING WITHOUT PURPOSE
- FATIGUE/SLUGGISHNESS

Fatigue/Lethargy - Lack of energy, weariness, decreased motivation

- FEELINGS OF BOREDOM
- FEELINGS OF BEING OVERLY "STRESSED OUT"
- LACKING THE INCENTIVE TO BE PRODUCTIVE

Guilt - Realizing or believing one has violated his or her own moral code; remorse

- FEELINGS OF CONFLICTION OVER ACTION OR INACTION
- RUMINATION ON ACTION OR INACTION
- COMPULSIVE THOUGHTS AND BEHAVIORS AIMED AT REPAYMENT

Shame - Humiliation; feeling of being improper or foolish

- FEELING INADEQUATE WHILE OTHERS "ARE PERFECT"
- CONCEALING FEELINGS OF LOW SELF-WORTH

Self-Loathing - Low self-worth; believing one can do nothing right

- CRITICIZING ONESELF FOR PERCEIVED FAULTS AND FLAWS
- RUMINATION ON PAST MISTAKES

Doubt - Lack of certainty; delaying action due to indecision

- DISTRUST IN CERTAIN INFORMATION
- LACK OF CONFIDENCE IN OWN ABILITIES

- FEELINGS OF PESSIMISM

Timidity - Uneasiness; lack of self-confidence; awkwardness

- FEELINGS OF SOCIAL ANXIETY
- LOW SELF-ESTEEM/SELF-CONFIDENCE
- CRIPPLING APPREHENSION

Unfortunately, these definitions are limited because words, themselves, are limited. Trying to explain emotion is like trying to scoop up honey with a net. The honey sticks to the web itself, but most of the real substance slip through the holes. The best you can do is to try to understand your own emotions on a personal level. There are two main methods for understanding emotions: psychologically and physiologically. Both your thoughts (conscious and unconscious) and your body contribute to how you feel.

Emotions and Your Body

Emotion is not just a psychological affair. When you react to internal or external stimuli, there are changes in your body, such as elevated heart rate, increased blood pressure, perspiration, or the release of a specific chemical, which can significantly affect how you feel. For example, when you are overly stressed, your body has a "fight or flight" response. A surge of adrenalin is produced by the body to prepare you to either face the situation or flee the situation, causing increased blood pressure, paling or flushing of the face, accelerated breathing, and other physical symptoms. If you've ever experienced an anxiety attack or panic attack, then you know how connected the mind and body are when it comes to emotions.

It's not only negative emotions that are linked to changes within the body. Many positive feelings are associated with certain neurotransmitters and "feel-good" chemicals. For example, a strenuous activity causes an increase in endorphin production, a hormone that reduces pain. Laughter also releases endorphins in the body as well as boosting immunity, decreasing stress hormones, and improving circulation and cardiovascular function.

Of course, physical symptoms of emotion are not always good or bad. There are some emotional symptoms that you may experience in both positive and negative circumstances. Increased heart rate

Emotions and Your Mind

Your mind is unique. There is no other psychological framework like yours, and you will experience emotions differently than anyone else. Take falling in love as an example. This may feel like weightlessness/lightness, or it may feel as if a million bees are trapped inside your stomach. It may be intense, or it may be subtle. It may be instantaneous, or it may emerge gradually. It is the same with anger, frustration, weariness, and even happiness. Just because you may not experience the same emotion in the same way as another person does not devalue what you are experiencing.

Because no two people will experience the same emotion in the same way, there is no definition that will be appropriate for every person. For example, two people battling depression may experience very different symptoms. The first may have trouble sleeping, have no appetite, and have no interest in things that were once enjoyable while the second has trouble with sleeping in too long, binge-eating, and intense waves of despair. These two instances of depression will look strikingly different from an external viewer, but both of these sufferers' emotions and experiences are valid and could be identified as depression.

This is why intense emotions like grief affect different people in such disparate ways. Two siblings facing the loss of a parent, for example, will each deal with it in his or her own way. The first may cling to family and friends for support in coping with the intense grief, while the other may become the family comic, cracking jokes to keep everyone smiling while dealing with the sadness in private. Neither of these responses is wrong; they're just different.

The trick is to stop comparing your emotional self to the emotional selves of others. Identifying and defining emotions in oneself must be a personal affair. When we compare ourselves with others, we end up invalidating our own feelings because they don't seem to "match what everyone else is feeling." Your emotions are yours, and they are valid already in the fact that you are experiencing them.

Understand Your Emotions by Sharing

One excellent way to better understand what you are feeling and where these emotions are coming from is to talk it out with someone you trust, even if that means you're sharing only with the blank pages in your journal. Try to describe what you're feeling. If it's anxiety that you struggle with, you may describe racing and unfocused thoughts, a hollow pit in your belly that persists for days, or an inability to sit still. If you suffer from depression, you may describe not being able to feel anything at all, known as apathy, or you may describe an intense and unrelenting sadness that makes you constantly want to cry. If you're overly stressed, you may describe feeling overwhelmed, or you may describe an inability to focus.

Whatever it is you're feeling, try your best to put it into words. The more you practice describing and expressing how you feel, the better you will understand your emotional self.

Try to give definitions to your feelings, even if there is no one word or phrase to describe it. Make a word up, or focus more on sounds than making sense, and say/write whatever rings true for you. If you can't articulate what you're feeling any more clearly than by letting out a guttural wail, then do it. Scream, cry, and wail— it doesn't matter so long are you are expressing yourself. Even if your name for your emotion only makes sense to you, being able to define it will give you power over it, and the more you practice expressing what you're feeling, the easier it will become. As you make your way through the rest of this book, you will learn how to cope with this complex and overpowering emotions, but the first step is identifying them.

Remember, emotions are a normal part of how we interact with ourselves and the circumstances and people who surround us. Having feelings is what makes you a human being. The problems start when emotions become destructive to our daily lives and our overall happiness.

Chapter 2. What Does Science Say About Emotions?

What do you typically do when your cell phone indicates a low battery? You absolutely charge it. When you comprehend that emotions are the only technique for correspondence between your cognizant and your intuitive personality you will discover understanding them turning into a simpler errand.

Emotions don't appear unexpectedly as certain individuals accept, however, they are automatically sent with a specific reason (perceive how to be responsible for your emotions) the wellspring of your emotions, and getting over undesirable ones.

Back to the cell phone example, what will occur in the event that you didn't charge the telephone? Or on the other hand, what will occur in the event that you cleaned it as opposed to charging it?

The issue won't be understood and the equivalent precisely occurs with your emotions when you don't react to the sign.

Rather than asking yourself where our emotions originate from, you ought to solicit yourself what's the reason for these emotions. When you comprehend the motivation behind an emotion, you will discover the message that your subliminal personality is attempting to let you know and you will most likely act accordingly.

On the off chance that you are feeling restless, at that point, react to that feeling by setting yourself up considerably more. In the event that you are discouraged, at that point, react to that feeling by bringing back expectations. In the event that you are envious, at that point, react to that feeling by showing a sense of fearlessness.

The best way to dispose of an undesirable feeling is to comprehend its source, the reason the subliminal personality is attempting to reach and afterward react to it.

The book *A Complete Manual for Getting Over Discouragement* was published without anyone else's input, the book gives a 100% certification to feeling better or you are guaranteed a full refund. 2knowmyself isn't a completely therapeutic site nor an exhausting one as a web reference book yet rather a spot where you will discover straightforward, to-the-point, and successful data that is upheld by brain science and displayed in a basic manner that you can comprehend and apply. From that book, we have a way to answer this fundamental question.

Emotions, similar to dread and love, are completed by the limbic framework, which is situated in the transient projection. While the limbic framework is comprised of various pieces of the cerebrum, the focal point of enthusiastic handling is the amygdala, which gets a contribution from other mental capacities, similar to memory and consideration.

Amygdala

Molded like an almond, the amygdala is in charge of numerous passionate reactions, similar to adore, dread, outrage, and sexual desire. Shippensburg University expresses that in creature studies, incitement or expulsion of the amygdala modifies the passionate reaction: electrical enactment causes animosity, while careful evacuation brings about aloof enthusiastic responses. In this way, harm to the amygdala can bring about irregular passionate reactions, and overstimulation causes unnecessary responses.

Hippocampus

The hippocampus is another piece of the limbic framework that sends data to the amygdala. One of the memory-handling focuses of the mind, the hippocampus collaborates with the amygdala when an individual has recollections with enthusiastic ties. The Canadian Institutes of Health Research includes that the association between the hippocampus and amygdala "might be the beginning of compelling emotions activated by specific recollections," which discloses enthusiastic reactions to horrendous recollections.

Prefrontal Cortex

The prefrontal cortex, situated close to the front of the head, is associated with basic leadership in light of emotions. The Canadian Institutes of Health Research expresses that the prefrontal cortex controls what choice an individual makes when they encounter a passionate response, and furthermore directs nervousness.

Nerve Center

The nerve center, likewise a piece of the limbic framework, encourages data into the amygdala. Shippensburg University expresses that the nerve center goes about as a controller of feeling, controlling degrees of sexual desire, joy, animosity, and outrage.

Cingulate Gyrus

The cingulate gyrus goes about as a pathway between the thalamus and the hippocampus and assumes a job in recalling passionately charged occasions. Shippensburg University takes note that the cingulate gyrus concentrates on the occasion, alarming the remainder of the cerebrum that is sincerely critical.

Ventral Tegmental Area

The ventral tegmental territory is additionally engaged with emotions and love, especially in how an individual sees joy. Dopamine pathways are situated in the ventral tegmental region: dopamine is a synapse engaged with disposition, and expanded levels hoist the individual's degree of delight.

Chapter 3. The Nature of Emotions

Emotions can be tricky. By understanding the mechanism behind emotions, you'll be able to manage them more effectively as they arise.

You must learn to let them pass without feeling the need to identify strongly with them. You must allow yourself to feel sad without adding commentaries such as, "I shouldn't be sad," or "What's wrong with me?" Instead, you must allow reality to be.

Typically, when someone is described as emotional, this is intended to be taken in a negative light. Emotional people are often regarded as impulsive, difficult to talk to, difficult to work with, unscientific, irrational, loud, or resistant to being spoken to. But this characterization is based on assumptions about emotional people. Indeed, labeling someone as emotional is a simple and almost devious way to neutralize and invalidate someone by immediately labeling them as something which they may or may not be.

At times, you'll feel disappointed, betrayed, insecure, resentful, or ashamed. You'll doubt yourself and doubt your ability to be the person you want to be. But that's okay because emotions come, but, more importantly, they go.

What Is the Ego

Your survival mechanism is not the only factor affecting your emotions. Your ego also plays a significant role in shaping the way you feel. Thus, to gain more control over your emotions, it is fundamental you understand what your ego is and how it works.

Now, let's clarify what ego means. "He/she has a big ego," refers to the ego as something close to pride. While pride is undoubtedly a manifestation of ego, that's only one part of it. You may show no pride and appear humble while still being controlled by your ego.

So, what is the ego? How was this identity created? Put simply, the ego was created through your thoughts and, as a mind-created identity, has no concrete reality.

As we'll see later in this book, attachment creates beliefs, and these beliefs lead you to experience certain emotions. For instance, you may become offended when people criticize your religion or attack your political principles.

Note that throughout this book, we'll refer to the ego as your "story" or your "identity" using these words interchangeably.

On the other hand, highly self-conscious people can see through their egos. They understand how belief works and how excessive attachment to a set of beliefs can create suffering in their life. In effect, these individuals become the master of their minds and are at peace with themselves.

Your Ego's Need for an Identity

Your ego is a selfish entity, only concerned about its survival. Interestingly, it's somewhat similar to your brain in the way it operates. It has its survival mechanism and will do whatever it can to persist. As with your brain, its primary concern is neither your happiness nor your peace of mind. On the contrary, your ego is restless. It wants you to be a go-getter. It wants you to do, acquire and achieve great things so you can become a "somebody."

As we already mentioned, your ego needs an identity to exist. The way it does that is through identification with things, people, or beliefs, and ideas.

Now, let's look at some of the things your ego uses to strengthen its identity:

Physical Items

The ego likes to identify with material things. It thrives in today's world. Perhaps, we can say capitalism and the consumer society we're living in today is the creation of collective egos, which is why it has been the dominant economic model in recent decades.

Marketers correctly understand people's need to identify with things. They know people don't just buy a product, they also purchase the emotions or story attached to the product. Often, you acquire certain clothes or a particular car because you want to tell a story about yourself. For instance, you may want to enhance your status, look cool, or express your unique personality, and choose the products most closely associated with these ideals.

Using things to create a story you can identify with is how the ego works. It doesn't mean things are wrong, per se. It's a negative issue only when you become overly attached to material things, believing they can fulfill you—which they can't.

Your Body

Most people derive their self-worth from their physical appearance. Your ego loves the way you look because it is the easiest thing to recognize and quantify. When you strongly associate with your physical appearance, you tend to identify more easily with physical and emotional pain. Believe it or not, you can observe your body without "identifying with" it.

Friends/Acquaintances

The ego is only interested in what it can get from them. In other words, the ego thrives on the way it can use people to strengthen its identity.

Now, let's see in more detail how the ego works in the following cases:

Parent/Child Relationships

Most parents' have a strong sense of attachment and identification with their children. This attachment is based on the false belief their children are their "possessions." As a result, they try to control their children's lives and "use" them to live the life they wanted to live when they were younger—this is called living vicariously through your children. You see this all the time. Next time you watch a junior soccer (or baseball) game, watch the parents on the touchline to see how some react. Try spotting the parents living vicariously—they are the ones screaming the loudest, and not merely in encouragement. This may happen mostly unconsciously.

Your Beliefs

Religion is a perfect illustration of the dangers of excessive attachment to beliefs. The ego will use any belief to strengthen its identity, whether these beliefs are religious, political, or metaphysical.

Other Objects of Identification

Now let's have a look at a (non-exhaustive) list of other things your ego generally derives its identity from:

- YOUR NAME

- YOUR GENDER

- YOUR NATIONALITY

- YOUR CULTURE

- YOUR PROBLEMS (ILLNESSES, FINANCIAL SITUATION, VICTIM MINDSET, ETC.)

- YOUR AGE

- YOUR JOB

- YOUR SOCIAL STATUS

- YOUR ROLE (AS EMPLOYEE, HOMEMAKER, PARENTAL STATUS, EMPLOYMENT STATUS, ETC.)

- YOUR DESIRES

The Ego's Main Characteristic

Here's the main aspect of the ego:

- THE EGO'S SENSE OF SELF-WORTH OFTEN DEPENDS ON THE WORTH YOU HAVE IN THE EYES OF OTHERS. YOUR EGO NEEDS THE APPROVAL OF OTHER PEOPLE TO FEEL VALUED.

The Ego's Need to Feel Superior

Here are some strategies it employs:

- **MANIFESTING AN INFERIORITY COMPLEX.** THIS HIDES A DESIRE TO BE BETTER THAN OTHERS. YES, EVEN IN THIS CASE, PEOPLE WANT TO FEEL SUPERIOR.

- **EXHIBITING A SUPERIORITY COMPLEX.** THIS HIDES THE FEAR OF NOT BEING GOOD ENOUGH.

- **LOOKING FOR FAME.** THIS OFFERS THE ILLUSION OF SUPERIORITY, WHICH IS WHY PEOPLE OFTEN DREAM OF BECOMING FAMOUS.

- **BEING RIGHT.** THE EGO LOVES TO BE CORRECT. IT'S AN EXCELLENT WAY FOR IT TO AFFIRM ITS EXISTENCE. HAVE YOU NOTICED THAT EVERYBODY, FROM ADOLF HITLER TO NELSON MANDELA, BELIEVES THEY'RE DOING THE RIGHT THING? MOST PEOPLE THINK THEY ARE CORRECT. BUT CAN EVERYBODY BE RIGHT?

- **COMPLAINING.** WHEN PEOPLE COMPLAIN, BY DEFINITION THEY BELIEVE THEY ARE RIGHT AND OTHERS ARE WRONG. IT WORKS WITH OBJECTS AS WELL. HAVE YOU EVER BUMPED INTO A TABLE AND COMPLAINED OR EVEN INSULTED IT? I HAVE, AND THE DARNED TABLE WAS WRONG TO BE IN MY WAY, WASN'T IT?

- **SEEKING ATTENTION.** THE EGO LIKES TO STAND OUT. IT LOVES RECOGNITION, PRAISE, OR ADMIRATION. TO SEEK ATTENTION, PEOPLE MAY ALSO COMMIT CRIMES, WEAR ECCENTRIC CLOTHES, OR HAVE TATTOOS ALL OVER THEIR BODIES.

Your Ego's Impact on Your Emotion

Understanding the way your ego works can help you better control your emotions. To do this, you must first realize your current story is the result of strong identification with people, things, or ideas. This intense identification is the root of many of the negative emotions you experience in your life. For instance:

- WHEN LIFE DOESN'T UNFOLD ACCORDING TO YOUR PERSONAL STORY YOU GET UPSET.

- WHEN SOMEONE CHALLENGES ONE OF YOUR BELIEFS YOU BECOME DEFENSIVE.

Chapter 4.   Emotions Influence

Using Your Body to Influence Your Emotions

Body Language and Body Posture

By changing your body language and your body posture you can alter the way you feel. When you are confident or happy you expand your body and make yourself bigger. Have you noticed how men straighten their backs, expand their chests, and tighten their stomachs when they see an attractive woman? That's an unconscious behavior designed to show confidence and power (the same way gorillas pound their chests).

In one of her experiments, Amy Cuddy, a social psychologist at Harvard Business School, noticed the following hormonal changes.

After adopting a high-power pose for two minutes:

- TESTOSTERONE INCREASED BY 25%.

- CORTISOL DECREASED BY 10%.

- Risk tolerance increased, with 86% of participants choosing to partake in a game of chance.

After adopting a low-power pose for two minutes:

- Testosterone decreased by 10%.

- Cortisol increased by 15%.

- Risk tolerance decreased, with only 60% of participants choosing to partake in a game of chance.

As you can see, you can actually change the way you feel merely by changing your body posture or facial expression. It is what some people call "fake it until you make it." For instance, you can put a smile on your face to make you feel happier. Conversely, you can negatively affect your mood and even create depression by changing your body posture.

The Benefits of Exercising

When the time came for David Kent to bring David K. Reynolds back to life, what do you think he needed to do? He needed to change his body position. Easy to say but hard to do when you're clinically depressed. Of course, he knew that better than anybody else. Still, he had to force himself to become physically active, despite not wanting to do so. As he started increasing his physical activity and getting busy, he felt better and better until he fully recovered.

David Kent's story shows that regular exercising improves, not only your physical well-being but also your mood. In one study, James Blumenthal, a clinical psychologist at Duke University, assigned sedentary adults with major depressive disorders to one of four groups: supervised exercise, home-based exercise, antidepressant therapy, or a placebo pill. After four months Blumenthal found that patients in the exercise and antidepressant group had the highest rates of remission. In his conclusions, he stated that exercise has more or less the same effect as antidepressants.

When he followed up with the same patients a year later, Blumenthal discovered that people who were still exercising regularly had lower depression scores than people who only exercised sporadically. Exercise seems to not only help treat depression but also help to prevent relapse. So, when it comes to mastering your emotions, make sure exercising is part of your toolbox.

Fortunately, you don't have to run ten miles a day to reap the benefits of exercise. Simply walking for thirty minutes, five days a week can work wonders. According to research published in PLoS Medicine, two and a half hours of moderate exercise a week could add three and a quarter years to your lifespan. Another study of five thousand people in Denmark showed that individuals who exercised regularly lived five to seven years longer than their sedentary counterparts.

The Benefits of Meditation

In Buddhism, the mind is often referred to as the "monkey mind," because, Buddhists believe human thoughts are similar to a monkey relentlessly swinging through trees. They are all over the place and never seem to stop. Meditation helps tame the monkey and cure it of restlessness. As you meditate, you become aware of the incessant flow of thoughts popping into your mind.

The Benefits of Visualization

Did you know your subconscious can't clearly distinguish real experiences from "fake" ones? This means you can trick your mind by simulating desired experiences through visualization. The more details you visualize, the more your brain will interpret the experience as real.

By using visualization to elicit positive feelings such as gratitude, excitement, or joy, you can condition your mind to experience more positive emotions, as we'll see in more depth in the section *Conditioning Your Mind.*

Using Your Words to Influence Your Emotions

Your words have more impact on your thoughts and behaviors than you might realize. Because your thoughts, words, and behaviors are all interconnected, they influence each other. For instance, when you lack confidence, you use certain words such as "I'll try," "I hope," or "I wish." Conversely, using specific words can make you feel less confident. This also means you can boost your confidence by using certain words such as, "I will." For instance, saying "I will change career," or "I will complete this project by the end of this month," will make you feel more confident than saying, "I hope I can change career," or "I'll try to complete this project by the end of this month."

To enhance your confidence, replace words that show self-doubt with words that display confidence as shown below.

Words to be avoided:

- "Would/could/should/might"

- "Try/hope/wish"

- "Maybe/perhaps"

- "If everything is okay…"

- "If everything goes well…"

Words to be used instead:

- "I will."

- "Absolutely."

- "Definitely."

- "Of course."

- "Sure."

- "Certainly."

- "Obviously."

- "Without any doubt."

- "No problem."

How Music Affects Your Emotions

We all know music affects our mood. Who hasn't listened to Rocky's song while working out? For instance, music can:

- HELP YOU RELAX WHEN YOU'RE TIRED.

- MOTIVATE YOU WHEN YOU'RE IN A SLUMP.

- HELP YOU PERSEVERE WHEN YOU'RE AT THE GYM.

- HELP YOU ACCESS FEELINGS OF GRATITUDE.

- PUT YOU IN A POSITIVE MOOD STATE.

Some studies have shown that listening to positive music can help people boost their mood. In a study conducted in 2012, participants reported higher positive mood after listening to a positive song for just twelve minutes, five times, over a two-week period. Interestingly, it only worked with participants who were told to make an effort to boost their mood. Other participants didn't report such mood improvement.

Valerie N. Stratton, Ph.D., and Annette H. Zalanowski, of Penn State University, also studied the effect of music on mood. They asked their students to keep music diaries for two weeks. Stratton concluded that: Not only did the sample of students report more positive emotions after listening to music, but their already positive emotions were intensified by listening to music.

Interestingly, the music genre and the context in which students listened to the music didn't affect the result. Students' mood improved whether they listened to rock or classical music, or whether they were at home, driving, or socializing.

Using Music to Condition Your Mind

Building playlists is time-consuming but well worth the effort. The world-class endurance athlete and coach, Christopher Bergland, uses music to help him stay motivated and perform at his best. This is what he wrote in an article published in Psychology Today.

Christopher enjoys listening to specific songs before a big interview or when he does public speaking. Personally, I like to listen to songs that make me feel grateful. What about you? How can you use music to improve your mood?

Exercise: Experiment with different types of music.

Experiment with different types of music and see how you can use them to boost your mood. For instance, you could use music to help you meditate, work out, or do your homework. As you do so, keep the following points in mind:

- **EVERYBODY IS DIFFERENT:** DON'T LISTEN TO A SONG BECAUSE IT'S POPULAR. LISTEN TO IT BECAUSE IT MAKES YOU FEEL THE WAY YOU WANT TO FEEL. WE ALL HAVE DIFFERENT MUSICAL TASTES.

- **KEEP EXPERIMENTING:** LISTEN TO DIFFERENT TYPES OF MUSIC AND SEE HOW THEY MAKE YOU FEEL. ARE YOU INSPIRED? MOTIVATED? HAPPY? RELAXED? START CREATING PLAYLISTS FOR SPECIFIC MOODS YOU WANT TO EXPERIENCE.

Chapter 5.   Bad Habits and Toxic People

Changing Your Emotions by Changing Your Behavior

We've seen you can influence your emotions by using your body, mind, or words. We've also discussed how you can change your interpretations of thoughts or events to change your emotional state. Unfortunately, when negative emotions suddenly arise or are too strong, changing your body posture or using positive affirmation might not be enough. In fact, trying to replace a negative emotion with a more positive one often fails. You cannot always overcome depression by cheering up or counteract grief by deciding to just "feel good." Neither can you expect profound sadness to disappear by repeating the phrase/mantra, "I'm happy, I'm happy, I'm happy."

However, you can influence the way you feel by changing your behavior. As you alter your behavior, your feelings will change accordingly. It may happen almost immediately, as when you distract yourself from mild anger by performing a task. Or it may take weeks or even months while you deal with profound emotions such as intense grief or depression.

To start changing the way you feel, whenever you experience a negative emotion, ask yourself the following questions:

- "WHAT CAUSES THAT EMOTION?"

- "WHAT CAN I DO ABOUT MY PRESENT REALITY?"

After asking these questions, identify concrete actions you could take to change your emotional state.

Example 1

If, after your boyfriend or girlfriend broke up with you, you keep remembering the good times you had together with sadness, it will take longer to get over the breakup. Although there is nothing wrong with feeling sad or remembering the past, if you want to move on, a better option is to avoid revisiting the past wherever possible. In this case, changing your behavior would be: Do your best to stop revisiting the old memories.

Example 2

If you constantly worry about an upcoming presentation at work, changing your behavior might be rehearsing your speech for hours. By doing this, you'll know the text so well you'll be able to perform well even under pressure. To give yourself an even better chance at success, you could also rehearse in front of your colleagues or friends.

Example 3

If you've been resenting a particular friend for weeks because of something they said or did, changing your behavior might be having an honest talk with them and share your feelings. This will allow you to clear the air, clarify any misunderstandings, and avoid building up resentment. Oftentimes, we misinterpret events or see things that aren't there.

Example 4

Sometimes, you feel sad, angry, or even depressed, and can't do anything about it. In this instance, the best you can do is to avoid focusing on your feelings, and just let them be. Your job here is to do what you have to do and live your life until these emotions fade. Don't forget to practice letting go of negative emotions as they arise. As you learn to detach yourself from the negative emotions, it will help prevent them from growing and becoming more entrenched.

Changing Your Emotions by Changing Your Environment

You cannot always control your emotions. Certain events, such as a breakup, the loss of a loved one, or severe disease, can trigger negative emotions.

However, you do have control over some events. Do you have daily life situations that affect your peace of mind? What if you could do something about them?

Sometimes, to reduce negative emotions you simply need to avoid putting yourself in the situations generating them in the first place. Perhaps, you watch too much TV, which makes you miserable. Or maybe, seeing your friends (seemingly) happy on Facebook makes you feel like a failure. Why not spend less time in such situations?

Example 1

Facebook was making me unhappy and I felt like a failure. People in my field were killing it and my friends looked so happy (or so I thought). Not to mention the fact I was wasting hours of my time mindlessly scrolling through my newsfeed. To overcome this drain on my emotional "bank," I drastically reduced the time I spent on Facebook. Ever since making the decision, I've been feeling better.

This example shows you that small changes can enhance your well-being. If you look at the things you do daily, you'll find activities or behaviors that don't support your happiness. Just removing one or two of these activities, or changing some of your behaviors, may noticeably improve your mood.

You may already know what you should do, but it's also possible you're unaware of the cost of some of your behaviors on your well-being.

Below, I've listed some examples of activities or behaviors that may rob you of your happiness. Ask yourself whether they're contributing to your overall sense of well-being:

- **WATCHING TV:** Although watching TV can be fun, it's also a passive activity that may not contribute much to your happiness.

- **SPENDING TIME ON SOCIAL MEDIA:** Social media is convenient and it allows you to keep in touch with your friends, but it can also be addictive. Facebook or Twitter can turn you into an addict craving the approval of others.

- **HANGING OUT WITH NEGATIVE PEOPLE:** People you hang out with have a tremendous influence on your emotional state. Positive people will lift you up and help you achieve your wildest dreams. Negative people will suck up your energy, demotivate you and destroy your potential.

- **COMPLAINING AND FOCUSING ON THE NEGATIVE:** Do you constantly see the negative side of things? Do you dwell on the past? If so, how does this affect your level of happiness?

- **NOT FINISHING WHAT YOU START:** Leaving tasks and projects unfinished in your personal and professional life can have a detrimental effect on your mood. Unfinished business clutters your mind. Feeling overwhelmed or demotivated is a sign you may have too many "open loops" in your life. Examples of "open loops" are unfinished projects you've been procrastinating over or avoiding people you need to talk to.

These are just a few examples. What about you? What activities or behaviors rob you of your happiness?

Conditioning Your Mind to Experience More Positive Emotions

You Are What You Think About Most of the Time

For thousands of years, mystics have told us we are the results of our thoughts. Buddha allegedly said, "What you think, you become." The essayist and poet, Ralph Waldo Emerson, said, "We become what we think about all day long," while Mahatma Gandhi said, "A man is but the product of his thoughts."

To take control of your emotions, it is essential you understand the role your thoughts play in generating emotions in general. Your thoughts activate certain emotions, and these emotions, in turn, generate more thoughts. Thoughts and emotions then feed each other.

For instance, if believed, the thought, "I'm not good enough," will generate negative emotions such as shame or guilt. Conversely, when you feel ashamed for "not being good enough," you'll attract more thoughts in line with that belief. You will focus on the things (you believe) you aren't good at or remember and dwell on past failures. This, in turn, will strengthen your erroneous belief.

Thoughts generate emotions and emotions dictate your actions. If you feel you don't deserve a promotion, you won't ask for it. If you believe a man or woman is "out of your league," you won't ask him or her out.

In a nutshell, this is the way thoughts work. They generate emotions that dictate your actions and shape your reality. While this may not be obvious to you in the short-term, in the long-term, you'll realize your thoughts have a tremendous impact on your life.

The Limit of Positive Thinking

Repeating to yourself, "I'm happy, I'm happy, I'm happy," all day long won't turn you into a living Buddha. You may benefit from it, but you'll still experience negative emotions. Unless you know how to deal with negative emotions when they appear, you'll fall prey to your own disempowering story. This story could be why you're such a loser or why *insert your favorite disempowering story here.*

Interestingly, people are often addicted to their story—even the negative ones—and are unable to let go of the "why," because they:

- ARE FUNDAMENTALLY FLAWED.

- WILL NEVER BE HAPPY BECAUSE *INSERT YOUR FAVORITE STORY.*

- AREN'T WORTHY OF LOVE.

- ARE NEVER GOING TO MAKE IT.

- WILL NEVER GET MARRIED.

Chapter 6. Use Your Emotions to Grow

As we learn how to regulate our emotions, we become more self-aware and understand how we can respond appropriately to given situations. Let's now look at some practical ways to use your emotional intelligence to improve your life.

Self-Management and Relationship Management

Managing emotions is a difficult skill to master. It takes a lot of time and practice. But once you're able to manage your emotions, then you can experience a freedom like no other. You have to find ways to manage your own difficult circumstances. That starts with how you deal with a negative emotion that might well up inside of you.

Pause Button

One of the things that therapists and psychologists teach in different classes for clients is how to hit the "pause button." This is something that stops a person from going off the edge and doing something regretful with their feelings. It is a simple concept, but it is not easily applied, because it is a challenge to put together. The pause button is something where the person stops himself, takes a deep breath, counts to ten, closes his eyes, and then looks the person in the face and responds to the situation. It can only take a few seconds, but it can make the difference between getting tangled up in a negative emotion or acting on it and responding the way you should. This powerful method has worked for many people and it can help a person regulate their emotions effectively.

Case Study

Eugenia was in the hospital for trying to punch other students in her school. She had gone into hallucinations and was feeling sick overall. She was a danger to those around her. Eugenia had a lot of problems with anger management, which made it difficult for her to control her behavior. As a result, she would get into a lot of trouble for fighting with other students. She wasn't a typical girl. She had some problems with her mental health. Moreover, she went to the psychiatric ward of a hospital to get the help that she needed. While in the hospital, she took a class about anger management and how to deal with the problems of issues that arise in our feelings. She learned about something called the "arousal pattern," in which our feelings can gradually flow up to the top like lava in a volcano that is waiting to explode. The key to managing negative emotions was to stop yourself before flying off the handle. To do that, people could use the "pause button" to stop themselves. At the moment, a person could stop and count from 1 to 20 and then look a person in the eye and talk after the pause. It was a way to stop a person from going off the edge and engaging in destructive behavior. Over time, Eugenia got better at this. She learned how to detect her arousal pattern and how to hit the "pause button" whenever she needed to. It helped her a lot.

Exercise

Another tool for self-regulation is exercise. When a person gets enough exercise, they will feel energized and able to tackle any situation. Think of a person who is a runner and goes out on a run. They may feel elated and happy after taking that run. If that person encounters a difficult situation, they might just simply want to put on their running shoes and go out the door. This will help them to regulate the negative emotions that can easily arise. Exercise is a proven method to beat the blues and to get a person out of a negative emotion. In addition to providing mental health benefits, it is also good for the body. If you can find a way to integrate physical activity in your life, you will find that you can maintain a lot more emotional stability, which will help your overall morale and enable you to do all the things you set out to do.

Case Study

Josh loved to go cycling. It was his hobby that he would do passionately. Although he had moments of distress at work and sometimes endured stressful situations, he knew he needed to get enough exercise to feel at his best. Sometimes, he would get depressed after having to deal with tons of work on his desk. When that happened, he would go out the door and go for a run or a bike ride, which would help him reorient himself. He realized that exercise was getting him into his happy place. He no longer needed to worry about his life. Every time he would go out and exercise, he would instantly feel better. Not only was it good for his physical health but also for his mental health. Cycling and running became his go-to therapy for whenever he felt depressed or stressed. In the end, Josh was able to manage his emotions well and leverage all the positive ones.

Mindfulness

Practicing mindfulness also enables a person to effectively manage their emotions, because it gives a person the ability to pause in the given moment, observe their surroundings, and think about their life. Mindfulness is a powerful self-regulation tool because it helps an individual to feel better and more relaxed in a given situation. It has helped when people practice mindfulness and meditation because it helps them to see things in perspective. Therefore, it can be of great help to a person who needs to learn how to regulate his emotions.

Relationship Management

In addition to self-regulation, emotional intelligence enables us to build relationships with the people around us. Often, we can leverage our own emotions based on what others around us are feeling. Having positive influences in our lives is one of the most important parts of living a good life. Without people who exude positive energy, we cannot accomplish the things we want to do. We will constantly be brought down by other people, who are always negative. The Negative Nancies and Neds in our lives are always going to tear down our emotions so that we feel bad about our lives and only want to complain about the circumstances that we are in. That is almost always counter-productive. Therefore, we need to find ways that we can cut ties with people who are negative and create bonds with people who have positivity and optimism. Only then will we experience greater emotional fulfillment.

If someone is not benefiting you in any way, you should cut ties with them. They may be a very negative person who is destroying your morale. You should say goodbye to them. Don't hang out with them anymore. Put a good distance between yourself and that person, because they won't be the one to build you up. Surround yourself with like-minded people, who are passionate about the things you love and can encourage you to be your best self.

In addition to setting boundaries between you and other people, you can also find ways to deal with emotional disputes that will undoubtedly arise. If you have a problem and different people have emotional reactions, then you can solve the problem through your own emotional maturity. By recognizing the emotions of other people, you can effectively end arguments and disputes.

Empathy

One of the most important things that you can learn is how to empathize with other people. It is vital that you understand where people are coming from and can see from their perspective. Empathy will shape your ability to relate to others and their emotions. It will also help you to develop your emotional intelligence. Find ways of connecting with others through empathy. You will see how you can understand the feelings and thoughts of different people. Ask someone, "How are you feeling today? Tell me more..." Invite someone into that space of vulnerability. It will change your life and someone else's, too.

Using Emotional Intelligence as a Guide in Decision Making

Another thing that we need to use our emotional intelligence with is decision making. Often times, we can be led to do things because of our emotions. We may experience something very strong within us that we cannot explain, but then we have to respond appropriately to that emotion. When we are aware of our own emotions and those of others, we can be guided to make the best decisions for everyone involved. We are no longer swayed by our own conflicting emotions.

When you use emotional intelligence in your decision-making, you are guided by objective ways of looking at situations. It's no longer about your feelings; instead, it is about how you perceive a situation through your EQ. When you look at it from this perspective, then you look at situations more holistically. Then, you consider all possible outcomes through the lens of EQ and considering other people in your life. You become less selfish and more aware of the individuals around you. This makes your relationships better and also gives you the ability to make more sound decisions about your own life.

For example, say you are in charge of a team of people and you have to watch over them to make sure they are doing their jobs. You recognize that they are struggling to meet deadlines, so you offer extensions and more support to them. It shows a lot of empathy for the people in your group. You no longer hold it against them when they don't finish things within the timeframe, especially if there is a rush job or some other task that requires quick work. Instead, you find ways to encourage your employees to do the best work they can. By offering continuous support to them, you make them feel more at home and they feel like they are valued as colleagues. By making your team feel better about the work they do, they will have more productivity and will produce the best possible work for your customers.

Using Emotional Intelligence to Improve Communication Skills

One of the ways that we can improve our communication skills is by using our emotional intelligence. Communication has the power to both create positivity and harmony with individuals as well as sow seeds of discord and resentment. The way we connect with one another influences the types of relationships we engage in. Therefore, it is crucial that we find ways of using effective communication to get our points across in ways that will bring harmony and agreement to situations. Many people are conflict-averse and don't like to have any kind of disagreement within a group. By communicating on the same level, you can find ways of bridging gaps, understanding individual differences, and come to points of agreement on different topics.

Effective communication, both in writing and in person, is difficult; however, it is something that can result in great relationships and bring out a lot of joy in people. When people can understand one another, then they will want to interact and get to know each other. They will build relationships and find ways that they can help one another out in different cases.

Emotional intelligence improves communication because it allows individuals to be aware of how their words affect others. When you are emotionally aware of those around you, then you will measure your words carefully. You will see how every word carries a certain weight with it and that you must be cautious to not disturb those around you. Sometimes, it is important to keep words to ourselves for fear of hurting those within our circles. It's not easy, especially if you want to express something. However, it can be helpful to hold things in that have the capacity to hurt others' feelings. We always want to be mindful of how others think and feel, because that will help us to get along with everyone around us.

Additionally, emotional intelligence helps us to be careful to promote peace within a group. It allows us to recognize when others are feeling tired, angry, or sad. When we can show that we understand how others feel, it also gives us a sense of trust. Others can be honest with us and show vulnerability. Emotional intelligence enables people to be their true selves with us because they have entrusted us with their lives.

Case Study

Jaric was active in promoting emotional intelligence in his company. He wanted colleagues to know how to interact on an emotional level because he knew that it would make them more successful. Moreover, he managed a team of individuals in his company. He wanted to communicate effectively with the team, but he also wanted to respect everyone's right to privacy. As a team leader, he decided that he would pick moments where he would communicate with all the members of the team individually. He knew how important it was to make sure everyone was on track. He would send DMs to every member and check in with them throughout the day. This made the members of the team feel valued and respected for their work. Additionally, he took care to avoid contacting anyone past normal business hours. He knew that some of the members of the team had families and children. Therefore, he didn't want to impede on their right to have their family time. Jaric was a respectful man, and he cared deeply about his employees. Because of his care for every team member, more people were staying on and there was less turnover because people were happy at work. They also had a healthier work-life balance. In the end, it was a great benefit to the company.

Chapter 7.   Negative Emotions

Jealousy

When you experience jealousy, you desire something someone else has, but you don't currently have. In this section, I will explain how jealousy works and provide you with some solutions to deal with it.

How to Use Jealousy to Grow

Jealousy stems from the belief you aren't good enough. You want something someone else has, believing that it would fulfill you. Alternatively, you're afraid of losing something or someone you believe is yours.

Jealousy Can Help You Find What You Really Want

Jealousy can let you know you're on the wrong path and can help you find out what you really want. For instance, in her book, *Quiet,* Susan Cain explained she would often feel jealous of her friends who were writers or psychologists. Interestingly, even though she was a lawyer at the time, she didn't feel jealous of successful lawyers—as her lawyer friends often did. This led her to realize she wasn't made to be a lawyer. As a result, she changed her career and became a writer.

I had a similar experience. While I was a consultant, I didn't envy or look up to successful people in my company. On the other hand, on my personal development journey, I became envious of successful personal development bloggers and YouTubers. I felt particularly jealous of two such people when I realized they were doing exactly what I wanted to do. This is why I created a blog and started writing books. As you can see, jealousy, when properly used, can be beneficial.

Jealousy Can Signal a Scarcity Mindset

In other situations, jealousy may indicate you're operating under a scarcity mindset. When I see bestselling writers, I sometimes become jealous. I feel as though they are stealing my piece of the pie, and I deserve success as much as they do. I'm not proud of this feeling, but I don't blame myself for having it, either.

This feeling of jealousy stems from the belief there is only a certain amount of success available out there. Thus, every time someone has a little success, they are stealing your piece of the action. Interestingly, this is often not the case. If anything, for writers the opposite is true. The more a writer can cooperate with other writers, the better chances they have to succeed. A writer who tries to do everything on their own is likely to fail. This is not limited to writers, of course.

Nowadays, when I see other writers having success, I remind myself what great news it is. After all, if they can do it, so can I. And the more successful my fellow writers become, the more they are in the position to help me in the future. This also works the other way around. The more I help other writers to succeed, the more they'll be able to help me in the future. Remember, what other people can do, you can do as well. Remember also, success is not a limited resource.

Jealousy May Tell You to Solve Self-Esteem Issues

Perhaps you're afraid your boyfriend or girlfriend may cheat on you, or leave you for someone else. This usually comes from the belief you aren't good enough, and you need your boyfriend or girlfriend to "complete" you. Unfortunately (or fortunately), the same way you can't control what people think of you or how they behave, you can't control your loved one's thoughts or behaviors either. Often, the very same desire to control your partner is what pushes them further away. While feeling jealous from time to time is normal, if you're excessively jealous, it is essential you look within yourself. Your insecurities and fears usually come from a lack of self-esteem and from the fear that you can't or won't be loved.

Jealousy May Lead to Some Behaviors

- **TRYING TO CONTROL YOUR PARTNER:** YOU MAY CHECK YOUR PARTNER'S PHONE OR EMAILS OR PREVENT THEM FROM GOING OUT TO SEE THEIR FRIENDS.

- **IMAGINING THINGS THAT AREN'T THERE:** YOU MAKE UP ALL SORTS OF STORIES IN YOUR MIND BY EXTRAPOLATING FACTS.

I invite you to refer to the section, *Not Being Good Enough*, to discover how to develop a healthier self-esteem.

Jealousy May Signal You to Stop Comparing Yourself with Others

From *The Power of Your Supermind* by Vernon Howard, we learn that jealousy often results from comparison with others. It is important to realize this type of comparison is generally as counterproductive as it is biased. Indeed, you seldom compare apples to apples. You look at some of your friends' successes, but you fail to realize this is only part of the picture. While they may seem happy and successful on the surface, it is quite possible they are unhappy or even depressed. The point is, rather than assuming your friends are happier than you are, it is better to assume that you are as happy as they are.

Also, guard against looking only at areas in which your friends seem to have it better than you. Perhaps, you focus on the fact they're making more money than you, or have a partner while you are single. Or perhaps you envy them for some of their natural strengths and abilities. The problem here is you fail to make an "apple to apple" comparison. You dismiss your own strengths or qualities which make you feel as though you're not as good as they are.

Even worse, you may often compare yourself with several other people. You look at areas in which they are successful and then you look at your own life to see how well you compare. Of course, not very well. How could you compete with the combined strengths of several people! Can you see how biased and unrealistic this type of comparison is?

The bottom line is, if you feel jealous, it may be because you engage in this type of unfair comparison. Instead, why not compare your "today's" self with your "yesterday's" self. After all, the only thing you can do is try to be better than you were yesterday, last month, or last year. Because we all start with different circumstances, skills, and personalities, there is no such thing as a fair comparison.

Exercise: Compare apples to apples.

This exercise will help you compare yourself to others more fairly.

Select someone you often compare yourself with.

Chapter 8.   Depression

Depression starts when you're not where you want to be in life, you have lost any hope to ever be, and can't accept it. This might happen after a tragic event in your life or more progressively as some aspects of your life slowly fall apart. Depression results from feeling hopeless in one or several areas of your life. Here are some examples:

- YOU LOST YOUR JOB AND HAVE NO HOPE OF FINDING A NEW ONE TO MATCH YOUR EXPECTATIONS.

- YOU'RE SICK AND HAVE NO HOPE TO RECOVER AS WELL AS YOU WOULD LIKE TO.

- YOU ARE DIVORCED FROM YOUR PARTNER AND CAN ONLY SEE YOUR KIDS ONCE IN A WHILE.

- YOU HAVE LITTLE HOPE OF FINDING A SUITABLE PARTNER.

- YOU'RE IN SO MUCH DEBT THAT IT SEEMS AS THOUGH YOU'LL NEVER GET OUT OF IT.

- YOU SUFFERED A BEREAVEMENT.

While the events above are tragic, depression can also be created out of more "ordinary," less severe events. For instance, some people may spend so much time dwelling on the past or worrying about the future they eventually become depressed. This may happen even though no significant events have occurred in their lives.

It is essential to remind yourself that depression, like other emotional states, is neither good nor bad, it just is. You are not your depression. You existed before it, you exist during it and, all things being equal, you will exist after it.

Depression Is an Active Process

While it may seem as though depression is happening to you, it is, in fact, created by the negative thoughts you identified with. Thus, you do have some responsibility in creating your depression. Does it mean you should feel guilty or beat yourself up for being depressed? Of course not! Never. In fact, you should never beat yourself up for any of the emotions you feel. That would be pointless. What it means, however, is that, because you've played a part in creating your current emotional state, you also have the power to get out of it. And that's great news, right?

David K. Reynolds' depression was entirely self-created (*Constructive Living*). It was an active process that involved adopting a certain body language, repeating certain words, and having certain thoughts. He had to act in a certain way to become depressed.

The good news is that because you have the power to "create" depression, you also have the power to climb out of it. However, in a negative state such as depression, ignoring negative thoughts and replacing them with more positive ones can be extremely challenging. Even if you try to think positive thoughts of gratitude, joy, or happiness, at first, they will seem to have no power.

But you may experience other negative emotions such as anger, for instance. You may ignore your anger at first. Your friends may even encourage you to do so—they would rather see you quiet and depressed, than angry. However, sometimes anger may help you move up the emotional ladder and overcome depression. Keep in mind, any emotions other than depression can help and learn to embrace whatever emotional state seems to give you more energy, and therefore, provide more power to move up the emotional ladder.

David K. Reynolds also suggests that feelings fluctuate over time even with depressed people. He wrote, "In the deepest depression there are ripples and waves of somewhat lighter moods." You can use moments when you feel slightly better to take whatever action may be beneficial to you at that time.

How to Use Depression to Grow

Depression is a sign you've lost touch with reality. Have you noticed that human beings are one of the few species on earth that have the ability to become depressed? This is because they are the only ones who can get lost in their mind and become enslaved by negative thoughts and disempowering stories.

Depression is a sign that you need to move away from your mind—by letting go of your worries about the past/future or your interpretation of the present situation—and reconnect to the present moment. It can be a powerful invitation to let go of the identity you've been clinging to for so many years. This identity is what led you to believe you should be doing certain things, making a certain amount of money, adopting a certain lifestyle, or developing a certain social status.

Depression invites you to reconnect with your body and emotions while getting out of your head. After all, didn't your mind create depression in the first place? Some people who experience severe grief, sadness or depression like to keep themselves busy to avoid thinking. When depressed, more thinking is seldom the solution. You rarely see people getting out of depression by using their minds.

Therefore, instead of thinking, you want to reconnect with your body. Exercising is a great way to do this and has been shown to be effective in improving your mood. (For additional information refer to the section *The Benefits of Exercising*.)

In some rare cases, severe depression can lead people to separate from their minds. When this happens, their story suddenly drops. Apparently, this is what happened to Eckhart Tolle as he recalls in his book, *The Power of Now*. He had a sudden awakening and his mind stopped.

In summary, depression tells you to let go of your ego and reconnect with reality. It makes you get out of your mind, which can only recall the past or anticipate the future, and live more in the present. Severe depression may require the help of a professional, but for milder depression here are some mediating strategies:

Exercise: Reconnect with your body and your emotions

To overcome depression, it is essential for you to escape your mind. It's easier to "feel" your way out of depression than to "think" your way out of it. I would venture to say that most people spend over ninety percent of their lives in their minds. They have only rare moments of lucidity when they are fully aware and present. For instance, they don't listen to people, but they:

- JUDGE AND INTERPRET WHAT THEY SAY.

- ANTICIPATE WHAT THEY'LL SAY NEXT.

- GET LOST IN THEIR THOUGHTS.

All these things happen at the "mind" level and show how people are not fully present. Things to do to reconnect with your body and your emotions:

- **EXERCISE:** AS PREVIOUSLY DISCUSSED, EXERCISING IS A GREAT WAY TO CALM YOUR MIND AND CONNECT WITH YOUR BODY, AND IT HAS A POSITIVE EFFECT ON YOUR MOOD.

- **MEDITATE:** MEDITATION IS AN EFFECTIVE WAY TO OBSERVE YOUR MIND AND STOP IDENTIFYING WITH YOUR THOUGHTS SO HEAVILY. MEDITATION IS SIMPLY A TOOL TO HELP YOU RECONNECT WITH REALITY BY OBSERVING THOUGHTS, EMOTIONS, AND SENSATIONS INSTEAD OF GETTING LOST IN YOUR MIND.

- ACTIVITY: GETTING BUSY ALLOWS YOU TO AVOID EXCESSIVE THINKING. INSTEAD OF FEEDING YOUR DEPRESSION WITH CONSTANT NEGATIVE THOUGHTS, CONCENTRATE YOUR ATTENTION ON SOMETHING ELSE.

- FOCUS ON OTHERS: AS MENTIONED IN DALE CARNEGIE'S BOOK, *HOW TO STOP WORRYING AND START LIVING*, ALFRED ADLER USED TO SAY TO HIS MELANCHOLIA PATIENTS, "YOU CAN BE CURED IN FOURTEEN DAYS IF YOU FOLLOW THIS PRESCRIPTION. TRY TO THINK EVERY DAY HOW YOU CAN PLEASE SOMEONE." WHETHER OR NOT IT IS ACCURATE, FOCUSING ON OTHERS CAN CERTAINLY HELP YOU FORGET ABOUT YOUR OWN ISSUES AND FOCUS ON SOMETHING MORE POSITIVE.

Unfortunately, when you feel depressed you won't want to do any of these things. However, as you start moving and start keeping yourself busy, your situation will gradually improve, and it will become easier and easier. Thus, it is important to take things just one step at a time.

Fear/Discomfort

Whenever we try something new, we experience anxiety. We are afraid of the unknown. This is why we like to maintain our daily routine and stay within our comfort zones. From our brain's point of view, this makes perfect sense. If our current habits allow us to be safe and avoid any potential threat to our survival (or the survival of our ego) why bother changing them? This explains why we often keep the same routine or have the same thoughts over and over. It is also why we may experience a lot of internal resistance when trying to change ourselves.

Thus, when we try to move beyond our comfort zones, we experience fear and distress. Now, do we want to stay in the same place most of our lives and avoid taking any risks, or do we want to pursue our dreams and see what we are truly capable of becoming? We have to remember, most of our fears are a threat only to our ego, not to our survival. Generally, they aren't physical threats, but imaginary ones. If we play it safe, we risk missing out on life, and we may regret it later.

Below are common fears you may experience:

- FEAR OF REJECTION: YOU'RE AFRAID OF BEING REJECTED. THIS MAY BE PHYSICAL REJECTION FROM A SPECIFIC GROUP, BUT IT IS GENERALLY MORE SUBTLE. FOR INSTANCE, YOU MAY BE AFRAID OF:

  - MAKING A COMMENT PEOPLE COULD DISAPPROVE OF.

  - ASKING SOMEONE OUT AND BEING TURNED DOWN.

  - SHARING YOUR WORK AND BEING CRITICIZED FOR IT.

- **FEAR OF FAILURE:** You're afraid of failing. This usually comes from the deepest fear of not being good enough; i.e., you are afraid of being ridiculed and believe that failure will erode your self-esteem.

- **FEAR OF LOSS:** Human beings have an aversion to losses, which is why we are often more motivated to prevent a loss than to secure a gain.

- **FEAR OF DISTURBING:** You're afraid of disturbing people. Perhaps due to the belief that you're not important enough. As a result, you may feel reluctant to affirm yourself for fear of appearing selfish.

- **FEAR OF SUCCESS:** You're afraid of success. You may worry you won't be able to sustain it with all the added pressure on your shoulders.

Chapter 9.   Procrastination

The lawn needs to be mowed, laundry needs doing, dishes are piling up in the sink. You want to eventually go out with your friends and also go grocery shopping. Don't forget the car needs an oil change and the dog needs a bath. We can put things off, saying we'll get to it tomorrow or I'll do that later. We're tired from a long day, hesitant. Putting things off is called procrastination, which goes hand in hand with depression and just being tired in general. People sometimes call this laziness.

Procrastination in moderation is okay. It's a habit we develop that comes along with our emotions. Sometimes we procrastinate because we really are very busy. Other times, it's because we can't make a decision, and don't want to hurt other people's feelings. Sometimes, not doing something is easier than doing anything. Vague plans or ideas are easier to ignore than specific deadlines and dates. When we are expected to be somewhere at a certain time, we have a harder time not showing up and so tend to be there. Procrastination is irrational, because we know we're engaging in avoidance behavior, and we are very aware we should do what we are avoiding. The theory is we avoid these tasks because we don't like the emotion that comes with doing them. But our ability to manage time and stay organized comes to naught when procrastination begins. Why would we want to do something that's not convenient to our mood? Opening the mail, calling that bill collector, checking our credit score -- these are events that make us vulnerable to depression, worry, anger, and most of all stress. We must gain control of this because procrastination only delays events that are inevitable.

You may feel as if you don't want to deal with the emotion behind it. You begin to feel like you're at a standstill. We are all creatures of habit in one way or another. Your everyday routine may consist of avoiding what you are putting off. Our biases tend to put our short-term urgencies up front, leaving the longer-term tasks for "the future." Once that "future" is the present, we find ways to continue to procrastinate.

Ask yourself what is the emotion behind the now-urgent task in front of you? what do you feel one you've put it off again? How do you feel the next day when you know you've put it off? When you think you have managed the task you've put off, you may feel more in control of your life, and you've avoided worry by not thinking about the task right now. Dishes and laundry always need to be done; you decide to choose one or the other depending on which is what is more important short term. Clothes for your appearance or dishes for meals. If you go for laundry, you've made the decision that your appearance is more important than food. And, you think you can compensate by using disposable plates or cups; if you do the dishes, you've decided you value your kitchen over clothing.

Multi-tasking is the enemy of procrastination; when we learn to multi-task, we tend to get more done. You could start a load of laundry if you have a washer and dryer at home, and while you wait for the clothes to get done, start the dishes. By the time the clothes are done, the dishes will be in the dishwasher. You take the clothes and put them in the dryer and while waiting for clothes to dry, you could find another task to stay busy with. The key is to not get comfortable or relax, because you might fall back to procrastination. If you relax, you might end up putting off getting the clothes out the dryer and think you did enough for the day so you'll fold them tomorrow.

If you don't have a washer and dryer at home, this is a little more difficult. It's more of a chore to gather your dirty clothes, the detergent and other cleaning supplies, quarters for the machine, and haul everything to the Laundromat and sit in a strange room while waiting for the clothes to finish. It's hard to get motivated for that. But here's a suggestion: Get a few plastic bags and put all your socks and underwear m in one, your shirts in another, and other clothes as necessary into as many bags as loads you plan to wash. If you don't have a dishwasher, start the water in the sink and let it run while you gather your laundry. Begin to scrub the easy dishes but let the really soiled ones soak. Now, you just have to rinse those clean dishes and set them to dry. Go to the laundry with your bags and put each bag into a separate washing machine. Put the clean clothes into three separate dryers.

You just did multiple tasks — you organized and categorized while you washed the dishes. This is training your brain to see how easy it is to do multiple tasks. How motivating is that! By the time you return with your clean, dried and folded clothes, the rinsed dishes are dry, ready to be put away, and the stubborn ones have been soaking, so are much easier to clean. You did two tasks and within that one task, you did two other tasks. You organized your clothes and categorized them in different bags.

You can do this same thing with most of your other chores. For example, you can text your friend and vacuum while waiting for a response. Start the laundry after you vacuum while you are texting your friend back. Don't be absorbed in just one task. Stay busy. Don't sit down and text your friend, because it might take your mind off what needs to be done. When you can balance keeping the mind busy when starting a task, and not think about the emotions behind it or the way it makes you feel, you can envision the reward for getting it out the way. Make a list of all the things you're putting off; see which ones can be done in tandem; this will take two chores off your list at one time, making things go much faster. Leave the list where you can see it, where it will taunt you if you try to ignore it.

Make a resolution and be sure to include a reward for finishing tasks – this motivates you and tricks your brain into wanting to do something. Rewards can be as simple as an hour of television after the chores are done or more elaborate, like a vacation after you've finished all the DIY home repairs. If you think of two chores as one, you get them both done and get to the reward much faster.

You can start this simple motivation exercise right now – and as with all skills, practice it every day until it becomes second nature. Don't let your mind talk you into procrastinating – think of the reward instead. Tell yourself now is the time to get this done. If you backslide, don't beat yourself up, but encourage yourself to want to get it done. Don't think about the dread of doing it; think about the reward after it's done. How would you feel if your boss had never looked over the resume you sent in? He would have never hired a great employee, right? I'm talking about you. If you don't look forward and move past this feeling of dread, the task will build up and you could lose out on great opportunities. You're climbing a mountain right now; your procrastination is the rocks building up to a giant rockslide threatening to send you back to the bottom. The more rocks you move out of the way, the faster you will get to the top and be able to see what is ahead of you.

I'm going to tell a short story and at the end of it, I want you to see how you relate to it and try to picture your own outcome.

It's the end of a great day. She gets home and sees all the chores still waiting for her: open the mail, do laundry, wash dishes, and organize the closet. She doesn't think about doing I, just sits down to watch TV. But there's nothing on, and her phone is dead. She looks around and goes into the kitchen for a cold glass of water. While she's standing at the sink, drinking her water, her eyes fall on the pile of dirty dishes. Why not wash some now, while she's standing here? She turns on the radio to listen to music while she washes. She then grabs her clothes and throw a load into the machine; turning the music up louder, she goes into her closet and begins to sort the clothes on the floor there. She puts aside the clothes she doesn't wear anymore, and bags them for the donation pick up. When she's done with that, she sees the clothes are done and puts them into the dryer. She finds a surprise in one of her pants pocket -- a five-dollar bill all wet and wrinkled up that she had forgotten about.

While the clothes are drying, she opens the mail – and finds several coupons she can use for groceries. She grabs the coupons and runs to the grocery store to get some dinner. Another surprise – she runs into a friend she hasn't seen in a while and they reconnect and exchange contact information. When she gets home, she has clean dishes to eat on and clothes to wear for tomorrow. She rewards herself by watching an old movie and having a glass of wine.

By not procrastinating, she managed to move her rocks to the bottom of the mountain; in return, she encountered more joy than she thought she would, including meeting her old friend. All this was a result of beating procrastination.

I don't know if you would like to do, this but if you would, go outside and get some rocks—four, to be exact -- and go to an open area where no one can get hit by the rocks you are going to throw. Pick up one rock and throw it far; wait for the sound of it hitting the ground or ripples in the water. You don't know where this rock went -- you know it went somewhere but cannot see it. Do it again; when you throw it say, "I'm doing this for my future." Don't wait for the sound or the ripples. Throw another one and say, "I can beat this." Throw another and say, "Now is the time." You're out of rocks. How does it feel? Does it matter where they went? No, they are gone, and they were just weighing your bucket down.

These rocks were your procrastination -- see how easy it was to get rid of them? And how good it felt to throw them? You can throw your tasks away by putting procrastination out of your mind and out of sight, just like those rocks you threw. Once you beat procrastination, your wilting flower will begin to come back to life. Don't worry about getting it done later -- get it done now! Tell yourself, "I will do this now." Don't let this behavior boss you around. You have to want this on your own terms for yourself, not for anyone else, and not because someone told you to do it. Because you told yourself to do it. You've read more than halfway through this book for a reason -- you chose it to master your emotions.

Chapter 10.   What Are Positive Emotions?

Before diving too deep into effective emotions, we should begin by ensuring we're all on the same page about emotions—and effective emotions mainly.

Advantageous emotions aren't truly "glad feelings" that we chase to feel short-term delight; just like the greater bad feelings, they play a vast role in normal existence.

There are many approaches to outline "emotion," however, they typically fall into considered one of two camps: Emotions are attitudes or responses to a state of affairs or an item, like judgments.

They had been called "multi-component reaction inclinations" that remained for a short period of time, roughly aligning with the second vision, and as mental stories that are each intense and fulfilling that adhere more to the first sight.

Whichever definition you think fits first-rate; the most important matters we want to recognize about them are:

- WHICH EMOTIONS THEY MAY BE.

- WHAT IS THEIR CAUSE OR FACTOR?

- HOW WE CAN ENHANCE OUR EXPERIENCE OF THEM, EITHER IN AMOUNT OR FINE, AND (D) WHAT EFFECTS THEY'VE ON US?

Examples of powerful Emotions

- "I LOVE BEING CONFIDENT."

- "I AM INDEPENDENT OF THE GOOD OR BAD OPINIONS OF OTHERS."

- "I AM BENEATH NO ONE AND NO ONE IS BENEATH ME."

- "I LOVE YOU…" (ADD YOUR NAME AND SAY IT WHILE LOOKING INTO YOUR EYES IN THE MIRROR, E.G. "I LOVE YOU, THIBAUT"). AWKWARD, ISN'T IT?

- "THANK YOU."

Exercise: Use positive affirmation for five minutes daily.

Notice words that show a lack of commitment, confidence, or assertiveness. Go over your emails before you send them and remove phrases such as, "I'll try," "I should," "I hope," etc.

Replace them with, "I will," or something equally assertive. For the next three weeks, challenge yourself to avoid using words showing a lack of confidence.

Additional tip: The world-famous life coach, Tony Robbins, has been using what he calls "incantation," for decades before meeting a client or holding a seminar. He uses both his body and certain phrases to put himself in the right state and to reach a level of absolute certainty. As you perform your own affirmations, try engaging your body as well. Remember, your words and your body affect your emotions.

Advantages of Mastering Emotions

If someone asked me to choose the single largest factor that contributes to a person's success in today's complicated and volatile world, I'd say emotional intelligence or the ability to control one's emotions without batting an eyelid.

Emotional intelligence is our ability to manage our emotions and those of others by discriminating among these feelings and using the information to guide our words, thoughts, and actions. To cut a long story short, emotional intelligence is an aggregation of your mental and emotional skills. Emotionally intelligent people enjoy a multitude of benefits in all spheres of life, including relationships, career, and social life.

Here are some ways your life can be impacted or benefited if you consciously focus on developing high emotional intelligence:

Greater Kindness in Everyday Life

One of the best benefits of high emotional intelligence is your ability to demonstrate more compassion for others both in your personal and professional sphere. This compassion allows you to connect with people at much deeper levels so you can forge meaningful relationships. Compassion can be manifested in several ways, including helping someone dealing with a personal issue by taking on their responsibilities or making small everyday decisions for the comfort/convenience of your employees.

Compassion helps you meaningfully connect with people both in your personal and professional life. You are able to reach out to people efficiently, forge more mutually fulfilling relationships, and create an atmosphere of harmony and productivity. Emotional intelligence awards you greater compassion in dealing with people in various personal, professional, and social scenarios.

Higher Employee Morale and Reduced Attrition

Morale may be an intangible concept in the corporate world, but its effects are highly measurable. You may not realize the value of high morale when it's there, but you will definitely know when it's missing. Think about the lateness, early departures, attrition, and sick leaves your company suffers from. When leaders take the time to build emotional intelligence and connect with their team members, it reflects in the employee's morale.

Emotionally intelligent leaders who build stronger emotional ties with subordinates witness improvement in the team's morale, lower measurable absenteeism, a higher team spirit, and a greater desire to contribute to an organization's success. The emotional intelligence skill-building cost can be minimal. However, the return on investment can be extremely high.

Let's get real here and call a spade a spade. Employees do not really quit roles, they quit senior managers. It is about escaping people and not positions. Emotionally intelligent leaders, who recognize emotional triggers, quickly pick up emotional clues of their team members, and "customize" their approach to each member's unique emotional make-up and motivation will experience greater success in retaining employees. This should not be mistaken for not doing justice to one's own voice or feelings. It simply means presenting an accurate emotional response towards each team member to treat them with greater compassion, respect, and empathy.

The problem with most managers who do not understand the concept of emotional intelligence is they use a one size fits all approach for dealing with all employees without understanding the emotional framework, motivators, and goals of individual team members. This one size fits all approach does not produce flattering results because personalities vary. Some people are more intrinsically motivated, while others thrive on extrinsic motivation. Some folks are quick to reveal their emotions; others aren't very comfortable sharing their feelings. Once you understand the emotional make-up of people, it becomes easy to deal with them more efficiently.

Increased Productivity

Emotional intelligence has a high correlation with an individual's work performance. Research has revealed that emotional intelligence is twice as crucial as technical/cognitive abilities, even among professions such as engineering. Emotionally intelligent managers, supervisors, and leaders are way more effective in managing teams, motivating people, and negotiating.

They create a more positive atmosphere with happier workers who are an asset to any organization. Happier workers translate into higher morale, low absenteeism, reduced attrition rate, and higher productivity. This leads to happier customers, more sales, and higher profits.

Thus, emotional intelligence is an invaluable trait when it comes to success in the workplace. While everyone within an organization possesses more or less the same technical competency and educational qualifications, only a few rise up the corporate ladder because of their ability to manage people and their emotions.

An emotionally intelligent leader who understands the true value of identifying and managing emotions can empower their subordinates with these skills on a daily basis. Discipline or self-regulation is essential when it comes to keeping your emotions in check, avoiding panic, remaining calm, and being an asset to the team.

Emotionally intelligent folks have little trouble recognizing and managing potentially destructive emotions that can create stress and lower productivity. The approach is calmer, more confident, and efficient. Rather than experiencing a touchier view, these folks depend on their ability to possess a more realistic view of themselves and others.

Awesome Communication Skills

People with a well-developed emotional quotient are more efficient when it comes to expressing themselves. They possess the ability to listen attentively to other people's verbal clues while also being able to tune into their nonverbal communication. They know exactly what to say to channel people's strengths. They use the right words and nonverbal signals to help people feel at ease. There is little scope for misunderstanding while communicating with a person who has high emotional intelligence.

Emotionally intelligent people are well aware of the most compelling emotional triggers of the people around them. They know exactly how to inspire people to act. People who are able to communicate by emotionally connecting with someone are far more effective than technically competent folks who fail to demonstrate empathy while communicating with people. Emotional intelligence awards you better response skills.

Dealing with Challenges

Don't you sometimes look at some people and wonder how they are able to stay afloat through the most challenging situations and emerge even more successful than before? Chances are, these guys score high in emotional intelligence. Emotionally intelligent folks have the ability to calm their body and mind to view things from a clearer and more objective perspective. Their acts are more mindful and less panic-stricken.

Greater calmness, objectivity, and clarity award you more resilience where life's challenges are concerned. Think about the Kung Fu fighter who can take on the most powerful opponents by constantly working on their martial arts skills. Emotional intelligence equips you with those skills to take on the toughest challenges that life throws at you with resilience.

Reduced Chances of Addiction and Emotional Disorders

Addictions are generally a direct result of our inability to cope with emotions. People who struggle to come to terms with their emotions use addiction as a mechanism to avoid the more underlying and deeper prevailing issues. When you fail to recognize and manage negative emotions, there develops an unfortunate pattern of dependency on external factors such as food, nicotine, illegal substances, alcohol, porn, and the like. Addiction is just a means to escape from emotions you aren't willing to deal with.

Emotionally intelligent folks are lesser prone to addiction because of their awareness of their emotions and their ability to manage these emotions. They have a solid understanding of their feelings and do not struggle to deal with them. Since emotional intelligence makes you happier, more confident, and balanced, there is a lesser propensity for dependence on destructive coping mechanisms.

They adapt more easily to challenges and changing scenarios in life. Emotionally intelligent people are competent in resolving differences and coming up with more positive solutions. Since they display such a high understanding of their own and others' emotions, it becomes easier for them to deal with conflicts.

Emotionally healthy people are less prone to be victims of drug abuse or binge eating disorders, which predominantly originate from much deeper psychological issues.

Better Leadership Skills

Emotionally intelligent folks possess a highly evolved ability to recognize and understand factors that drive others, which makes them amazing leaders. They are able to make the most of this invaluable information to strengthen their loyalty and forge stronger relationships with people. A competent leader is intuitively tuned into the most compelling aspirations and desires of their followers. They know the "hot buttons" of their employees and exactly how to channelize these "hot buttons" to increase overall productivity and positivity within the work environment.

Emotionally intelligent leaders know how to channelize this information for extracting better performance/productivity from people and keeping them happy. People with a high emotional quotient excel at recognizing the strengths and weaknesses of people and harnessing an individual's virtues for benefiting the team.

High emotional intelligence creates better leaders who are able to inspire greater faith and loyalty by using their teams or followers or emotional range. They are more aware of their emotions, which allows emotionally intelligent folks to create a harmonious environment. Practicing emotional intelligence makes you a better leader.

Did you know 67% of all competencies said to be fundamental for high performance in the professional sphere is emotional intelligence? Take the example of the world's most successful CEOs. Amazon's Jeff Bezos passionately talks about getting right into the hearts of his customers in a 2009 YouTube video while announcing the company's Zappos acquisition.

Emotional intelligence helps in building emotional maturity, boosting social intelligence, preventing relationship problems, enhancing interpersonal communication, helping control emotions, dealing with stress, influencing leadership, helping authorities make sound business change decisions, supporting staff, and controlling resistance to change.

Chapter 11. Theories of Emotions

For centuries the classical view of emotions was widely accepted as clear and concise. This first theory states that emotions are the result of neurons being triggered by something that has happened to you, suggesting that emotions are expressed the same and viewed the same from person to person. This classical view of emotions is set on the belief that you are not only born with these basic emotions and the ability to express them but that you can automatically recognize these emotions in other people from birth.

After much research and a deeper understanding of emotions, how they are expressed, and the factors that affect one's emotional response, this classical view has been rejected. While some of this view may be correct, such as being born with certain emotions, most of it is greatly disputed and has been proven to be flawed. When psychologists began to explore this notion of recognizing emotions based on facial expressions, they began to unravel the deeper complexities that surround emotions and our ability to distinguish them within ourselves, as well as identifying them in others.

The idea that each basic emotion has a set of emotional patterns—a sort of fingerprint—was the basis of the classical view of emotions. Each emotion has a pattern of physical changes a person should experience regardless of age, race, gender, or any other factors. By recognizing the changes in a person's face, body, and brain, emotions could be identified. The classical view of emotions suggests that facial expressions are a key factor in determining and recognizing the emotions we feel. Unfortunately, because of how many muscles are found in the face and how even the slightest movement can show a different emotional reaction, many studies on facial emotion recognition reported that many individuals say they are feeling one way while their facial muscle movement indicates a different emotional state.

This understanding that the natural facial expression of emotion may be understood by most individuals, such as a smiling face often means a person is happy, it is much more difficult for individuals to actually read a person's face. For example, when asked to give a happy face, angry face, or scared face, you might exaggerate your facial expression more than if you were naturally feeling these emotions. When you naturally express these emotions, your expression can often show surprise, disgust, boredom, or anxiousness. When individuals are asked to identify the emotion that matches the facial expression, they are often always wrong. This leads to having to explore what more can be understood—not only in how we express our emotions but also in how we read these expressions in others.

The six main emotional theories that try to better explain and understand emotions have elaborated on specific responses and factors that cause them. These theories fall into three main categories: physiological, neurological, or cognitive. Physiological theories refer to theories that associate emotions with responses in the body, neurological theories are those that suggest emotions are the result of brain activity, while cognitive theories propose emotions occur because of thoughts and mental perceptions.

Evolutionary Theory of Emotions

Charles Darwin, who focused much of his life on the idea of evolution, also tried to explain emotions through an evolutionary process. His evolutionary theory of emotion suggests that humans developed emotions as a form of survival. Love evolved in humans as a way to better reproduce, and fear evolved out of the need to better protect themselves from danger. This theory points to how emotions serve a strictly adaptive role. This has allowed humans to gain a better understanding of other people's emotional responses, as well as the way animals display emotions in order to avoid danger, find safety, and increase their chances of survival.

James-Lange's Theory

William James and Carl Lange are responsible for creating the James-Lange physiological emotional theory. James was a psychologist and Lange a physiologist, and both suggested that emotional reactions are determined based on the physiological reactions generated from an external factor. With this theory, it is not your emotion that results in your physical reaction to situations, but instead that your physical reaction to a situation causes you to think you are feeling an emotion. When you begin to tremble in an unfamiliar situation, you will most likely conclude that you are experiencing fear.

Cannon-Bard's Theory

Walter Cannon created a physiological emotional theory that opposed the James-Lange Theory, pointing out how we can experience emotions prior to having any physical reaction to those emotions. Cannon noted that many physiological reactions can occur without feeling any emotions, like how a racing heart could simply be because of physical activity as opposed to linked to the emotion of fear. He also determined that emotions arise too quickly to be the result of just a physical response to a situation.

Though Cannon's theory was first revealed in the 1920s, it was expanded on in the 1930s by another physiologist by the name of Phillip Bard. The theory highlights how the brain is able to receive messages at the same time. These messages trigger a physiological as well as an emotional response to an outside factor. These responses occur at the same time, and neither occurs as a result of the other.

Schachter-Singer's Two Factor Theory

Schachter-Singer's theory is a cognitive theory stating that a physiological response must occur before an emotion is experienced. But it is not just the physiological response that causes the emotion—once a reaction occurs, the individual must then be able to identify what triggered the response and be able to label it appropriately as the emotion they are feeling. This theory relates to both James-Lange and Cannon-Bard's theories. The theory accepts that a physiological response causes an individual to feel a certain emotion, as does James-Lange's theory. It also supports the fact that many physiological responses can be interpreted as a wide range of emotions, based on the situation. The key difference is that Schachter-Singer's theory bases the type of emotion that is experienced as a result of the cognitive interpretation one goes through before labeling the emotions.

Lazarus' Cognitive Mediational Theory

Also known as the cognitive appraisal theory, Lazarus' Theory is based on the notion that one must be able to think through the situation they are present in. When you are able to see the relationship between your thoughts and the assumptions you make about a situation, you can then begin to understand what is affecting your emotional responses. This theory focuses a great deal on better understanding stress—how individuals react to stress and what causes them to feel more stress in one situation over another. This theory pointed out the assumptions we make about certain situations, whether based on truth or not, have a significant impact on the emotions we experience.

Facial-Feedback Theory of Emotion

This theory emphasizes how your facial response has an impact on your emotional response. Therefore, if you force yourself to smile in a situation that you find unpleasant, you will eventually feel more pleasant emotions. This theory began to highlight how emotional response may be controlled if we change our approach to how we behave and react to these emotions.

The Theory of Constructed Emotions

The theory of constructed emotions presented by Dr. Lisa Feldman Barrett is a newer look of emotions. This theory disproves any previous ideas, notions, assumptions, and theories we have held onto for centuries. Instead of believing emotions are part of human hardwiring, physiological reactions, or even universal, it looks at emotions as concepts. This theory considers how the brain process information it receives in every second of every moment, categorizing and labeling it according to past experiences. This makes it easier and quicker for the brain to identify whatever you may encounter.

The brain categorizes how your body is supposed to react when certain emotions arise. It also forms predictions as to how or what you might feel and begins to prepare your body to react in the appropriate way. These predictions are also based on past experiences—in a sense, your brain is recreating how you felt and how your body responded to situations in the past that are similar to the situation or event you are about to encounter. This is what causes your body to have physical reactions because your brain is signaling these reactions to occur to cope with the experience, like how you begin to cry when you are sad. Crying is a natural calming mechanism for the nervous system.

Unlike many of the other theories here, this theory suggests your emotions are not a reaction to the situation you are in but instead a result of the brain's prediction of what may occur. Sometimes, these predictions can be wrong, in which case the brain can either take in additional information from the senses and adjust the prediction or it can stick with the original prediction despite new information contradicting the past experience. Your brain recalls the past experience in such a way that not all the information may be present. It would be as if you are seeing images in strictly black and white, but when you look at the image in full color, you have a clearer idea of the original picture. When you look at the black and white image, you can see what the figure is and where it begins and ends. This is how your brain recalls emotions. It gives you the black and white concept it has stored, then matches it with the current colored situation, allowing you to react in accordance with both the past and present information aligning.

The theory of constructed emotion also brings light to a better understanding of how the range of emotions one can access. Emotional granularity is explained as to how well you are able to read your internal states of emotions. This relates to how much of an emotional range you have. When you have a better understanding of more emotions, as opposed to just feeling good or feeling bad, you have a higher emotional granularity. This allows you to better understand and express your emotions because you give your brain more information and data to pull its predictions from. It also allows you to better identify cues to accurately describe which emotional state you are in. Having a higher emotional granularity will result in being able to face more challenges in life.

Each of the theories explained offers a better understanding of how emotions arise, what can influence them, and how the brain identifies them. These theories can all be called upon to better understand your emotions.

Chapter 12.   What Impact Your Emotions?

What impacts emotions? This is a valid question to ask if you want to understand and master your emotions. From the context of this chapter, we will be looking at two important things that impact emotions; the brain and social norms/culture.

The brain is a grand master in manipulating emotions so even when you think you know the source of your feelings or emotions, it could be really tricky. We like to think we are in control of our feelings and the triggers behind these feelings, but the truth is our brain has a much more profound impact than people like to admit.

Every single moment, there are lots of activities going on in your head and the brain is at the center of all these activities and somewhat complex processes. A lot of process is involved in how we interpret situations and react to them. Remember that emotions are defined by three important things: cognition, responses, and reaction. The brain determines every of these activities which makes us wonder how our brain actually impacts our emotions. What happens in your brain right before you experience an emotion?

The first thing to know about your emotions is that it starts right from the brain. Emotions are a combination of our feelings, the way we process these feelings, and our responses or reactions to those feelings. The primary purpose of emotion, according to Charles Darwin, is to encourage seamless human evolution. In order for us to survive, we have to pass on our genetic information from generation to generation which is why emotions are important. Recognizing the important of emotional experiences, the brain takes it upon itself to evaluate stimuli and activate a suitable emotional response to it. The brain reflects and considers the best way to respond to a situation so that the primary purpose of survival is achieved and then, it activates a suitable emotion as response so as to propel the rest of the body to react accordingly. So, when you find yourself reacting to a situation with a kind of response, that is actually your brain triggering the emotion it considers right for your survival right at that moment in time.

The brain is a vast network of complex processes which include information processing. One of the brain's primary networks contains neurons which send signals from one part of the brain to the other. Now, these cells or neurons transmit signals through what we call neurotransmitters; some kind of chemicals we either receive or release in the brain. The neurotransmitters are what make it possible for one part of the brain to communicate with another part. Dopamine, norepinephrine, and serotonin are some of the most examined neurotransmitters. Dopamine is the neurotransmitter that has to do with feelings of pleasure and rewards; it is the chemical which makes you happy when you do something good. This neurotransmitter is released as a reward for you to give a pleasurable and happy feeling. On the other hand, serotonin is the neurotransmitter linked with learning and memory. It is believed to play a critical part in brain cells regeneration and research has shown that an imbalance in serotonin can lead to an increase in stress, anger, anxiety, and depression. Norepinephrine on its own helps modify your moods by controlling the levels of stress and anxiety.

Now, when there is an abnormal or unbalanced release and processing of either of these chemicals, there is usually a very profound impact on your emotions and emotional state. For instance, when you do something that requires dopamine to be released and sent to the part of the brain responsible for information processing but your brain doesn't process or receive the dopamine as it should, it could result in you feeling sad or mildly unhappy. Therefore, the abnormal release and processing of dopamine, serotonin, and norepinephrine has immense impact on the emotions you have and the responses you give to certain situations. The next time something which should have made you happy gives feelings of sadness, remember these neurotransmitters.

Again, your brain exerts influence on emotions because it is central to how emotions are formed. The brain consists of different parts that are all responsible for generating different emotions. The part of the brain responsible for processing emotions is the 'emotional brain' which is generally referred to as the limbic system. In this limbic system, we have the amygdala which, as we have said in a previous chapter, helps you measure the emotional quality or value of a stimulus before initiating an appropriate response; it is the part of the brain responsible for initiating the fight or flight response. The hypothalamus helps you regulate your responses or reactions to emotional triggers. There are also other parts of the brain like the hippocampus which all impact your emotions due to its memory retrieval functions. In fact, the hippocampus determines your emotional responses to triggers. Since different parts of the brain process different types of emotions using different methods, damage to any part of the brain can have a huge influence on your emotions and moods no matter how mild. Central to all of this is the limbic system which takes a generalized and simple approach to stimuli.

The brain's left and right hemispheres also play important roles in emotion and responses. The hemispheres are responsible for keeping you functioning but they also play a part in how you process information. The left hemisphere deals more with concrete thinking while the right hemisphere concentrates on abstract thinking. Because they both process information in different ways, the left and right hemispheres work together to manage emotions. While the right hemisphere identifies an emotion, the left hemisphere interprets the emotion. For instance, when the right part of the brain identifies an emotion like anger, it alerts the left brain which then makes a logical decision in interpreting the context of the emotion and deciding the appropriate response to give. This is actually all a synchronized system but if something goes wrong and one hemisphere can't do its job properly, it affects how you react to basic emotions. For example, if the right brain doesn't identify a negative emotion like it should, it prompts the left brain to become overwhelmed with the emotion without knowing how to respond.

Memory whether long-term or short-term is the function of the brain and our memories dictate and inform our emotions. You get angry when you recall a resentful memory and get happy when you remember a pleasant memory. This is a continual process in the brain; it identifies a past emotion and then places you in a mood based on the emotion. So, when next you get angry without knowing why, it may be your brain recalling some painful memory to initiate a negative emotion. How you can override this is to push yourself to think of things that have made you happy in the past. For example, if you are sad, simply thinking of some happy memories can trigger the release of dopamine which rewards you with feelings of happiness.

Sleep

When do you struggle with sleep the most? It is probably the times you had so much on your mind, and rest seemed to be a far-fetched idea. Anxiety and negative emotions can cause a person to become restless, and this has adverse effects on sleep patterns.

Quality sleep is one of the prerequisites for a healthy body, and when your body is deprived of sleep, it can create a ripple effect that affects you mentally and physically. Sleep loss affects your attention span. You will realize over time that you don't pay enough attention to your work or what others say to you.

Sleep deprivation also prevents the body from strengthening its immune system with the cytokines needed to fight infection. When you don't have enough cytokine in your body, it will take a longer time for you to recover from illnesses.

Anxiety, worry, fear, panic attacks, and sadness are some of the negative emotions that affect your ability to sleep peacefully daily. If you don't find a way to manage such feelings, you will be dealing with more problematic health and physical issues.

Sports

This has been proven to be true over a series of studies. So, if you want to put your feelings in check, stay away from junk food, eat balanced meals, and maintain a good routine of exercise.

Keeping your feelings in check overtime can be tough. This is why many persons do not make much effort and give up eventually. Sometimes, you will lose the plot, but this should not deter you from moving on.

A person who can manage effectively manage his emotions and put his feelings in check will be viewed as one with logical reasoning, an effective conflict handler, a person with high emotional intelligence, inner peace, and self-confidence.

Food And Drinks

When a person is dealing with negative emotions, food is usually the last thing on their mind. Not eating may or may not be intentional in that state. But anxiety always paves the way for eating disorders, and this is true because most people who are diagnosed with eating disorders struggle or may have struggled with stress in the past.

Eating disorders are illnesses. The people who experience them observe a sudden change with eating, which is usually caused by their anxiety over weight gain and how they look.

Music

Art is a great way to use non-verbal expression to increase your mental well-being. Art is a magical carrier of emotion for humans; we tend to use art to understand the world and make sense of it. This is not the only function of art, however; there are many functions. One is dancing; others are relaxation, grief, mourning, celebration, and war-rousing. There are many functions of music, and nearly all of them our emotions. Music is a great example of an art form that can transform the emotional experience and bring about emotional awareness. If a person is sad all day, and goes to work, comes home, eats dinner, and watches a movie before going to bed, with no other consideration, they are just keeping that sadness inside. You have to do something about it to deal with emotions, and learning to deal with emotions only learned after a person is able to identify their emotions it is the first step on the path to self-realization.

Relationships

Once you've raised your social awareness skills and learn how to understand what other people are feeling, you are ready to work on maintaining your relationships. Let's clear it from the start – this is not an easy job. You will need to use all other areas of emotional intelligence to help you build and maintain them.

Four Things You Need to Know

The first thing you need to assess and manage is the effect different people have on you, as well as recognize what they are feeling and what is the cause that they are feeling that way. If you fulfill that, you will be able to make a decision on the best way to communicate with them to achieve the result that suits your or their needs.

Four different criteria determine the effectiveness of managing relationships:

- DECIDING WHICH COURSE OF ACTION IS THE MOST APPROPRIATE FOR A GIVEN SITUATION. TO DISCOVER THIS, YOU WILL NEED TO

- INTERACTING WITH THE OTHER PARTY BASED ON YOUR RESEARCH
- THE RESULT IS WHAT SHOULD GUIDE YOU TO CHOOSE WHAT TO SAY AND HOW YOU WILL COMMUNICATE YOUR MESSAGE. THAT MEANS THAT YOUR ACTIONS COME WITH A PARTICULAR GOAL IN MIND, MAKING MANAGING YOUR RELATIONSHIP AN INTENTIONAL ACTIVITY
- YOUR NEEDS WILL BE WHAT WILL CAUSE YOU TO WANT A PARTICULAR OUTCOME. IT MIGHT BE YOUR PERSONAL NEEDS OR THE NEEDS OF YOUR BUSINESS

Seven Competencies

Certain competencies might be best related to workplace relationships, but they can also be applied to relations outside of work. The reason you might primarily connect them to your office is that they have a lot of similarities with leaders.

Goleman defined the competencies, and they include:

- INFLUENCING – THE ABILITY TO PERSUADE OTHER PEOPLE INTO DOING SOMETHING THAT FITS YOUR, THEIR, OR JOINT NEEDS
- INSPIRING – THE SKILL TO MOTIVATE OTHER PEOPLE BY INSPIRING THEM

- DEVELOPING – THE ABILITY TO GIVE USEFUL FEEDBACK AND HELP OTHERS BUILD THEIR KNOWLEDGE AND SKILLS
- BEING A CATALYST FOR CHANGE – KNOWING WHEN CHANGE IS REQUIRED AND STARTING THE PROCESS
- MANAGING CONFLICTS – THE ABILITY TO EFFICIENTLY SETTLE OR MISUNDERSTANDING, DIFFERENCES OF OPINION, OR DISPUTES
- CREATING BONDS – BUILDING NETWORKS AND MAINTAINING THEM
- COLLABORATING WITH OTHERS – CREATING EFFECTIVE TEAMS AND NURTURING THEM

You can use each of these competencies to maintain your relationships. However, before you do that, take some time to think about them.

The question you should ask yourself is "Do you perform these competencies right now and are you good at them?"

It's always a good idea to write everything down. Think about various areas of each competency and note what you are doing well and what can be improved. For example, providing feedback for other people is something that you surely do right now. On the other hand, you can also write where you could use some improvement (yes, it might be the same competency, just a different area).

The next step is to think of two actions that you will take to develop yourself in that area and write them down. Taking an online course, conducting your own research, reading a book, or trying to mirror the behavior of someone you respect are all included. Finally, try to actually perform these actions and work on your competencies. You will notice that it will improve managing your relationships with others.

Let's take a look at the example of giving feedback. You are already giving it to other people, but you would like to work on it and make it more supportive. You conduct an online research and discover some tips and try to apply them the next time someone asks you for feedback. You will notice that they will more appreciate the feedback that's supportive and constructive and your relationship will benefit from that.

Work Environment

For emphasis, it is not possible to eliminate all difficult situations because of the nature of human interactions and the need to take risks as well as adventure. There are also external factors that are beyond the scope of individual control. Avoiding circumstances that trigger adverse emotions is among the effective ways to condition the mind to handle setbacks. An example is where an individual feels irritated when a deadline is fast approaching. It might help if the person started planning and working earlier by splitting the work into modules. One can go further and inform colleagues that short deadlines may make the person react adversely. Change the environment where possible to get away from triggers, especially where the triggers are non-human entities. The bottom line is to ensure that the mind is prepared and has little pressure when handling a challenging issue.

It is important to learn to change thoughts. It might appear an easy strategy, but most people struggle to let go of their thoughts. As indicated earlier, thoughts impact emotions and subsequently, emotional reactions. The persistence to current thoughts occurs because the mind is trying to solve pending issues, and this is sometimes useful. Through the use of cognitive reappraisal, one can replace adverse thoughts with constructive thoughts. Sticking to negative thoughts could also be linked to low self-esteem.

Words That We Use

You cannot take words back, so when you are about to use abusive words in a fit of anger, rest assured they will go a long way to harm the person you are saying them to. You can say you don't mean them later, but the words have already had their effect. Sometimes the use of hurtful words stems from a desire to make them feel the hurt you're feeling, but it's not necessary.

Positive/Negative Thoughts

The way you interpret different situations is highly influenced by your emotions. When you are excited, you are more likely to view situations with optimism, while sadness brings about fear and pessimism. Reflect on your emotional filter and take a more realistic stance by reframing your thoughts.

Restructuring your thoughts involves embracing a more positive outlook when pessimism sets in. Not all situations will present itself with the same level of ease. Something's, all you need to do to step back, look within, isolate your emotions, so that you can have a clear line of thought. While more is required, the bottom line is to stop ruminating on negativity. You will easily lose control of managing your feelings. You can embark on activities that will switch the channel of negativity in your brain, such as taking a walk and running a chore.

Review this book

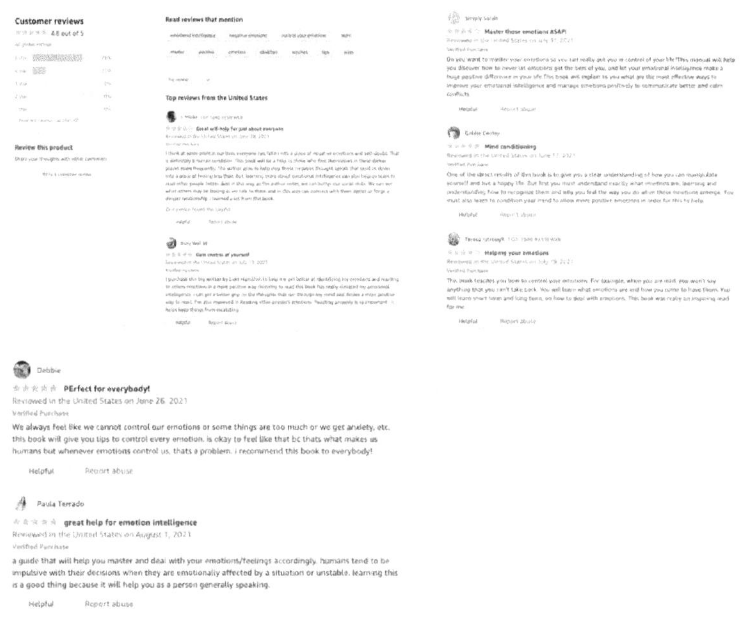

Thanks for reading so far! I would be extremely grateful if you would take 1 minute of your time to leave a review on Amazon about my work.

Click here to get your feedback or frame the QR Code with your smartphone

Conclusion

It is my hope and pleasure that you have taken your precious time in reading this book. It is also my hope that you have enjoyed reading it. The book, *How to Master Emotions*, introduces you to the cruel world of emotional feelings that have cropped in our life, devouring every bit of human beings. The book also forms part and parcel of your daily emotions and how you might, in the end, reduce negative emotions.

One of the aims of this book is to give you a clear view of how you can manipulate yourself and live a happy life. That's a life that is not being distracted by negative emotions. In every situation, our feelings are affected by egos. Everyone in life has an ego; however, to some, it is not well displayed. The ego has a more significant impact on our lives, especially when it comes to our emotions. Getting away to handle it will not only help you but also initiate a happy feeling in those around you. Therefore, to manage all these, then you need to concentrate on chapters dealing with the effects of ego and how it can be achieved.

On several occasions, our emotions are influenced by many things, which later on might get reflected in our daily activities. The impacts of these factors on our feelings might lead to severe suffering or elements of pain. However, some effects might create the right environment towards the realization of abilities to manage our emotional life. Your emotions are affected by breathing, music, and even your body. Again, it is also affected by sleep and even your thoughts. For you to live a better life where emotions will never be an issue, then you need to take control of all these. The good way to do so is to get yourself once more in these various chapters dealing with this. Therefore, you have the key to your happiness.

The main objective of this book is also to help us change our emotions so that we can be more productive and lead a healthy life. Changing your feelings involves several factors. Therefore, it may include changing the way you live things, conditioning your mind, and also being in a position to change your behaviors. If, in any case, you have a negative emotion, then you need to look for ways to establish a change for the betterment of your life.

The book, *How to Master Emotions,* talks much about several emotions that we need to grow. Some of these emotions are seen as negative emotions in various contexts. However, if you want to succeed in life, then these emotions should be instilled in you. Being defensive, jealousy, depression, forgiveness, anger, and rage are a few examples of emotions that you have to emulate and live with them. Others include gossiping and even screaming at people. All these have the power to increase your happiness and gives you a productive life. The best thing to do here is to take a quick look at the various benefits of all these negative emotions and traits and use them to better your life.

Fortunately, nothing is as sweet as getting a solution to something that has been bothering you most of the time. In this case, the universal occurrence of negative emotions that has threatens our life in all perspectives. These emotions include anger, frustrations, depression, and even anxiety. The book gives out clear guidelines on how you can eventually deal with your negative emotions. You must, therefore, concentrate on these chapters so that you will be able to have full control of your negative emotions. I know the book has created solutions to your impending troubles with your feelings. I also know that the book has been very informative and educative. If so, then it is my kind request that you may find it well with you to make reviews of the book, *How to Master Emotions,* on other sites.

By understanding some of the special kinds of feelings, you can gain deeper information about the way those feelings are expressed and the impact they have got on your conduct. It's very hard to keep in mind but, no emotion is an island. Instead, the various feelings you revel in are nuanced and complex, operating collectively to create the wealthy and varied cloth of your emotional existence. There has never been a greater hobby in high-quality emotions and their effect on our lives—and for accurate purpose! Anxiety and overthinking aren't always scientific circumstances, however, a natural emotion is crucial for survival while an individual finds themselves dealing with risk. An anxiety ailment develops whilst this reaction becomes just too much to handle.

Keep a watch out for new effective emotions, and you'll be keeping up with a vivid and vibrant region of studies. Being a distinctly emotional man or woman is like being caught on a roller coaster—it has its "ups" and "downs." Feeling more than others is both a blessing and a curse, however, it's you—if you could learn to live with it (and be happy about it), so can others!

www.ingramcontent.com/pod-product-compliance
Lightning Source LLC
Chambersburg PA
CBHW061812250726
48657CB00001B/397